Hope on the
Border
~~~~~

Hope on the Border

~~~

*Immigration, Incarceration,
and the Power of Poetry*

~~~

by
Seth Michelson

Morehouse Publishing
19 East 34th Street
New York, NY 10016
www.churchpublishing.org

Morehouse Publishing is an imprint of Church Publishing Incorporated

Cover design by David Baldeosingh Rotstein
Designed by Stefan Killen
Typeset by Nord Compo

ISBN 978-1-64065-839-4 (hardcover)
ISBN 978-1-64065-840-0 (eBook)

Library of Congress Control Number: 2025934366

Printed in Canada

— for my sons, Ilan and Joaquín,

and
for displaced people everywhere;
may you always find
peace and a home

*That they walk, even stumble, among us
is reason to praise them.*

— THOMAS LUX

*If oppression returns again and again,
so too does resistance.*

— MARTÍN ESPADA

Contents

Introduction

Thank you for opening these pages. Herein many desperate people are eagerly awaiting this chance to connect with you from around the country and the world. Most are children, reaching out to you from isolation cells inside a maximum-security juvenile immigration detention center in the United States. But there are also adults in refugee camps, in legal clinics, and in immigration detention centers, including women in the largest immigration detention center in the United States designed specifically for family detention, meaning mothers with their children, who are as young as six months old.

Regardless of age, gender, nationality, or location, these people have all suffered tremendously, and their suffering continues, even as you read this. Still, they fight to maintain hope not only for themselves but also for humanity. And that is what they wish to share with you: a message of the resilience of hope in the human condition. Against all odds and despite ferocious setbacks, these people continue onward, hoping for brighter days and believing in the goodness in human beings despite brutal personal histories.

Still they dream of futures full of love, safety, and peace. And why not? Those are common human wishes. Plus, as asylum seekers, these are tremendously accomplished people. They have escaped grave danger in their countries of origin, and they have survived grueling transnational treks, often alone and penniless, in a willed effort to change the conditions of their lives, and perhaps those of their families. As evident in their success in reaching the border, they possess remarkable vision, determination, courage, and ingenuity, and they can achieve wonderful things in this world if given the chance. After all, they've already faced down hunger, homelessness, exposure, and destitution. They've persevered through robberies, beatings, kidnappings, extortion, rapes, stabbings, gunshots, torture, and incarceration. And they've braved all kinds of discrimination, whether misogynistic, homophobic, transphobic, racist, xenophobic, or otherwise. And still hope courses through their veins.

Their hope is both a source of sustenance for them and a call to action for you and me. It has helped them to cope with enormous suffering, and it can inspire others to think and act too. We can listen to and support these people, if we so choose. We can hear their stories and become their active allies, standing beside them in a fight for a better future, much to the betterment of all of us.

So my hope with this book is that you'll hear the hope of these many different people. I hope it will inspire you to support them in their journeys, and to affirm with them a fundamental belief in the dignity of all human beings.[1] I hope, too, that it will inspire you to join movements advocating for the just treatment of all people. It is among the most basic tenets of our pact as a species today that we will not intentionally hurt, enslave, or cause the death of one another.

If successful, these chapters will leave you feeling well-informed and empowered to act with empathy, insight, and reason. We are better than our current border policies and politics, which misrepresent our spirit and cause terrible violence. Moreover, when we act maliciously towards others, we hurt ourselves too. As the renowned human rights attorney Bryan Stephenson puts it, "We are all implicated when we allow other people to be mistreated."[2]

It bears mention, too, that the notion of hope in this book is as complex as it is nuanced. In its simplest form, it is the stubborn human hope born of a brute faith in being alive. This is the ancient hope of Ecclesiastes, for example: "For to him that is joined to all the living there is hope" (Eccles. 9:4, KJV). In more modern terms, it is the hope that Nelson Mandela writes of to his wife, Winnie, from prison, saying "hope is a powerful weapon even when all else is lost."[3] And this bedrock hope in continuing to live even when all else seems lost is the steel in the foundation of the lives of the refugees in this book, and ours too.

Throughout this book you will also encounter an important, pragmatic form of hope. It, too, might be familiar to you: it is the hope in fighting for justice.[4] It is the hope in working purposefully each day to build a better future, however arduous the labor. It is this hope that the celebrated poet and activist Gloria Anzaldúa celebrates when exhorting, "Do work that matters. *Vale la pena*."

We might simply agree that we want a nation that actively works to diminish human suffering and thereby enhance our collective well-being. And to do that, we must help the most vulnerable among us. As Dr. Martin Luther King, Jr., explains so poignantly, "[l]ife's most persistent and urgent question is, 'What are you doing for others?'"[5] And it is in that spirit that I hope you'll read this book and connect deeply with the people in it.

The future of our nation depends upon it.

CHAPTER 1

~~~~

So It Begins

*Word and form will be the plank on top of which
I shall float over billows of silence.*

— CLARICE LISPECTOR

I magine with me: it is 8:15 a.m., and class is beginning.
The room is bright with fluorescent light and packed with
students. But despite our many bodies, the room is cold this
December morning. We're in rural Virginia, tucked away in
a remote nook in the Blue Ridge Mountains. Outside snow is
falling in silence on pine trees. Inside it is so cold that most of
the students are sitting huddled on their seats with their knees
tucked up and under their sweatshirts for added warmth. And
warmth is what we're after.

For this is no ordinary group of students. They're young
teens incarcerated in the most restrictive maximum-security
detention center in the United States for undocumented, unac-
companied youth. Herein each child is held in a small, concrete
isolation cell while indefinitely awaiting the adjudication of
their immigration status by a federal judge.[1]

In the meantime, they struggle through their arduous
days.[2] As is well documented, self-harm is common, and suicide
attempts are all too frequent.[3] Children arrive at class here

5

with bandaged wrists, scabbed necks, and bruised bodies and hearts. Through and against all of their suffering, we gather like this weekly, to read, write, and discuss poetry.

With each visit I lead three poetry workshops on three separate cellblocks. The administrators assign me to the three cellblocks that they deem most appropriate for me that week, whether for reasons of security, availability, health, or staffing. And sometimes I arrive to turmoil. For example, after President Trump won the 2016 election, the children rioted in desperation, understanding that his politics would mean a more painful and violent future for them.

Regardless of the cellblock where the workshop occurs, the children are consistently amazing with me. They are peaceful, trusting, and vulnerable, and each workshop buzzes with their creativity, candor, and courage in writing and in conversation. In this manner, they convoke for themselves through our time together far more than a collaborative space for the sharing of creative writing. They also create a nourishing, alternative *community* for themselves within the circumscribing oppression and violence of life in the detention center.

The children cherish the countercultural space of the workshop. In it they can see, hear, and embrace one another, working together in a spirit of solidarity and collaboration as artists, not detainees or inmates. In this manner, they pen and share poetry each week through their sweat, agony, and hope, arguing for their humanity in a system dehumanizing them at every turn.

Such is the case this cold December morning on Cellblock C. The children are in high spirits, even before we begin our literary activity. At the table nearest me, a group of boys hover over their seats in a dilated moment before sitting, joking with one another in sarcastic comments and friendly nudges and pokes the way teens goof around in every high school cafeteria or classroom, as they settle in. Just now Eduardo is teasing Aldo about his hair, which the former thinks is hilariously wild and unkempt. Aldo retorts by shaking his long, tight curls in Eduardo's face like a Portuguese Water Dog shaking off the rain.

I survey the rest of the room and nod and smile in silence until every child is watching me. I then propose the theme for today: a meditation on poetry itself. I ask them to call out, as boisterously as they'd like, their definitions of poetry, whatever they may be. It is a tough ask, as I openly admit to them in the ensuing seconds of silence while the children take seriously the weighty challenge. I ask it differently: "Can we write poetry in here together if we can't define what poetry is? What exactly are we doing each week?"

I know I am pushing them. Some are as young as twelve, and few are older than sixteen. But I believe in them. So I also ask them to really think, and if willing, to share aloud what they are thinking. Ideas begin to trickle in. Poetry is fun. Poetry is playing with words. Poetry is rap. Poetry is our experience. Soon they are vibrantly conversing, and I guide that loosed energy towards individual writing.

"How is poetry an *activity* as much as a literary genre or a concept?" I ask.

The children catch on, pick up their stubby, two-inch rubbery pens, and begin to explore in writing their ideas of what and how poetry *is*.

"Be reckless with your imagination," I urge after a few moments of silence, but for the footfall of the booted guard wandering among their tables. "Be as fully present on the page as possible."

The resulting writing is exquisite. If read blindly in a magazine or book, these poems would scarcely reveal that these poets are children, or that many of them are illiterate or can barely read. Nor would a reader immediately surmise that the poetry comes from a workshop on a maximum-security cellblock lined by isolation cells.

Take for instance Yelson's *ars poetica* titled "La poesía" ("Poetry"). A quiet boy with deep brown, pensive eyes, he writes in an almost indecipherable scratch of phonetically spelled syllables, and with no space between words. Of course, neither handwriting nor literacy mean anything in the context of poetry, which springs from every human being. One simply needs the luxury of the time and energy to write it down or speak it. Here is Yelson's poem and translation.

La poesía

*La poesía es una forma de explicar tus sentimientos
a tí mismo, otra persona o muchas personas, una
manera de liberarte de las cadenas que te atan a
la dura realidad. También la poesía es un tipo de
descripción que define quién eres y serás en la vida.*

Poetry

Poetry is a form of explaining your feelings to
yourself, someone else, or many others, a way of
freeing yourself from the chains that tie you to
harsh reality. Poetry is also a kind of description that
defines who you are and who you will be in life.

The children love it. They clap for Yelson and immediately begin to praise his poem. The conversation eventually keys into the final sentence with a special verve. When I ask them to explain more specifically why they like these lines in particular, they testify to their hope. They like how poetry can help you to be "who you will be in life," not who you are. In other words, it helps them to see a future beyond the degrading agony of life here in detention. They also speak of how much they enjoy writing about who they are striving to be in the world, and how they want to live. With time running out, I pass out jelly beans, reminding the children that good writing can be sweet in our mouths. I leave them happily chewing and head to the next cellblock.

~~~~~

I shudder to think how our workshops in here exist only by the merest chance. I began them in the fall of 2015, thanks to a passing comment many months prior by an acquaintance in a casual conversation at a social event in a different town. I was new to the region, and offhandedly, that person alerted me to the very existence of the detention center. I would come to learn that it had traditionally kept a low profile in this very conservative, rural area, which might otherwise object to the importation-for-profit of undocumented children from Latin America into their backyard.

Regardless, that chance conversation quickly ramified into many more on the topic, and with multiple pertinent people. Via their insights and generosity, I eventually was able to broker a meeting with the administrators of the detention center. I had taught poetry in prisons since my twenties, and I had been a poet and poetry professor for decades. Still, as I dressed for that meeting in front of the mirror above my bathroom sink, I remember my nervous breathing while buttoning my white dress shirt, tying my blue-and-white-striped necktie, and donning the jacket of my gray suit. My nervousness lay not in my ability to lead the project, nor to describe it adequately to others, but in the possibility of failing to convince the administrators to give me the chance to work with these children. I knew they would flourish in our collaboration if given the chance, but I had also been warned not to get my hopes up about workshops because of the institution's reputation as a very strict federal facility. And I would be asking them to try something uncharacteristic and unprecedented in their extreme confines.

Leaving my house in my suit and tie, a final, steaming mug of coffee in hand, I begged the clouds for the administrators to green-light the project. As I drove to the detention center, I rehearsed my most salient points again and again. Soon I was sitting in the large, austere office of the executive director, explaining those points in person to him and to one of his senior administrators.

I began by offering myself to them as a free resource. I did not want budgets to disallow our opportunity. So I emphasized that I required only the time of the staff and the children, and I quickly added that I would arrange, too, for any and all materials necessary for each visit, whether poems, pens, or writing journals for the children. Appealing to administrative worry, I then detailed how these literary activities could help not only the children, but also the staff. I explained how an entire cellblock would typically fall into a low-stress, calm, and concentrated hush during my workshops due to the typically rapturous engagement of the incarcerated young writers.

At this point I saw the administrators glance at each other, and their eyes looked intrigued to me. But their faces remained stoic and hard to read. I pushed on with my pitch, explaining how a typical workshop might operate logistically. I emphasized not only the practical components of safety and industry, but also the propensity for the experience to cultivate joy and pleasure in the participants across the meeting. I also expressed a hope to publish the children's poetry bilingually so as to share it with readers beyond our workshops. And I tried to reassure the administrators of our high probability of success. I offered my decades of experience with running successful poetry workshops, whether in universities or far beyond them, including in such diverse places as community centers, prisons, public and private schools, nonprofits, geriatric homes, and more, and not only across the United States but also the world.

With our meeting concluding, I quickly added that I was bilingual in Spanish; held a bevy of advanced degrees in poetry; was a professor of poetry at a nearby, acclaimed university; and had published multiple books of poetry, as well as book chapters, articles, and essays about poetry. I mentioned, too, that I was a globally sought poet and speaker. It was an embarrassingly self-indulgent rush of language that contradicted my shy and self-effacing personality. But it was strategic: I did not want my personality to obstruct this possibility for the children.

As I recollected my poise, the administrators and I bid farewell to one another with smiles and handshakes. I crossed my fingers to hear good news. By chance, the stars aligned, and I was invited a few weeks later to begin both the institutional and the federal training necessary to volunteer inside the detention center.

Throughout that training, which often occurred one-on-one due to the relatively nonexistent roster of volunteers awaiting these permissions here, I listened attentively, learning in great detail about the children, the infrastructure of the facility, personal safety inside and beyond it, and matters of institutional and national security. And soon I'd been approved as a volunteer and found myself standing for the first time in the midst of a group of boys and girls on Cellblock B.

For this first visit, I was accompanied by several curious administrators of various ranks and offices and an extra guard or two. I was also acutely aware of the many locked doors beyond me, the isolation cells, and the cameras constantly surveilling us for guards in distant booths. Amidst all of this, it came as no small relief to me when the children took with immediate delight to our project.

In fact, the children jumped right in, and they have been vibrantly writing poems and commenting on them on every cellblock in here ever since. More deeply, they seemed to harbor a special penchant for producing powerful verse, almost effortlessly. They certainly agonized over memories, language, and the conditions of captivity, but poetry flowed from and through them. Perhaps it was attributable to their deft ability to blend precocious and brutal life experience with our literary conversations about technique, practices, and genre. Perhaps they are an especially talented group of writers. Regardless, I especially admired their skill in tenderly nurturing one another through writing and conversation. That, too, inspired me to exhaust myself in their service as I prepped and led each workshop on each cellblock before racing off to teach two or three different courses back-to-back at my university, an hour's drive away.

And who wouldn't commit similarly to these children after hearing them read aloud their poems in workshop, like the following one?

Estar aquí
Estoy agradecido por:
el futuro porque quizás puedo cambiar mi vida
a otra mejor,
espero quedarme aquí para cambiar mi vida.
Poder aprender inglés y estudiar y mejorar.
Encontrar amigos buenos.

Being Here
I'm thankful for:
the future when I might be able to change my life
for the better,
I hope to stay here so I can change my life.
Learn English and study and better myself.
Make good friends.

I love this poem for reminding me of its author, Javier. He is a slender young teen put together delicately but with a fierce optimism about the future. He is well liked by his peers for his easygoing nature and his soft-spoken, sincere participation in our workshops.

More broadly, Javier's poem reminds us that each of these incarcerated young refugees is in many ways like any child you could meet. Don't all children dream of learning and of living fabulous futures? Don't all children want and need to make good friends?

Simultaneously, though, these incarcerated boys and girls are also unlike most children. They have endured far more pain than most. They have endured more punishment, despondence, and isolation. Yet still they radiate gratitude, when they feel safe enough to share it. They radiate hope. They each dream of a better future, which we could offer to them.

Instead, they have been so dispossessed, disempowered, and dehumanized that they do not even control their own names. For example, they voted unanimously for their names to appear in print with their poetry, and they signed consent forms to permit it. However, that was overruled by a joint decision of the Department of Justice (DOJ) and the Department of Homeland Security (DHS), forcing me to change their names herein.

Despite their imposed anonymity, the children remain ardent advocates of my sharing their words and experiences.

In some ways, it exemplifies their unyielding hope to surmount their greatest fear in detention—being erased from existence and forgotten forever. Such is their daily existential terror in being housed in isolation cells.

One spring morning, a child named Adrián wrote remarkably about this. It happened in a workshop that I had designed precisely to help them to explore this fear. My hope had been for our shared process to support the children through pedagogy in trauma writing, with the writing prompt creating a forum for them to articulate and discuss the fear, if they wished, and with a group of understanding and empathetic peers. Ideally, such self-expression and exploration would assuage a smidge of their anxiety, pain, and terror, even if only for the duration of the workshop. Here is the poem.

Olvido
Sin razón de existir
siempre olvido que soy
real y esto hace que
me duela el alma
que no tengo o que
ando por algún lado
y no me encuentra.

I Forget
Without reason to exist
I often forget that I am
real and this makes
the soul that I don't have
ache as if
I'm walking somewhere
unable to find myself.

After hearing this evocative poem read aloud in that work-shop by Adrián, the room fell silent. There was a stillness that felt taut and minutes long, despite likely being no more than ten seconds. At that point, another boy, Josué, found the courage to be the first to respond to the poem and poet. With a sad smile, he offered a warm compliment, intimating in hushed, colloquial Honduran Spanish that he understood and shared Adrián's feelings of desperation in being forced to endure the agony of life in here day after day.

As is typical in workshops, that first response encouraged more. Soon everyone was discussing the poem in thoughtful detail, poring over its depiction of the children's all too familiar sense of the painful solitude of life lived in isolation. Our conversation progressed into a debate about how they might endure it better. We wondered aloud how they might keep one another from reaching the breaking point of wanting to harm themselves, like one member of the group whose wrists were freshly wrapped in medical gauze, and another whose neck was wreathed in scabs.

Quite poignantly, too, Adrián clearly felt heard and embraced by his peers. He listened attentively to their every comment, not saying a word. He was being nourished by their empathy the way a flower absorbs sunlight on its face. He was taking in their insight, understanding, and eloquence, and in the process, he seemed to me to grow an inch or two taller in his seat.

Simultaneously, I do not wish to imply here or anywhere that poetry or workshops have resolved anything for these children. Their suffering is as relentless as it is agonizing. More practically, they live in constant fear of being deported. Every last one of them has credibly asserted to me, and to many other adults, that deportation would condemn them to lives of poverty and violence on the streets of their respective countries of origin in Latin America. And at least one of the children was murdered shortly after being deported to his natal country, just as he had predicted in US immigration court, where a federal judge denied his pleas for the safety of asylum here.

Still the children come to our poetry workshops with hope. They come with trust and vigor. However grueling their daily lives are in detention, they somehow manage to write and share with vulnerability and composure. Maybe it is their need to be heard and understood. Maybe it is because they want to feel accepted into a community, which the workshops offer. Maybe it is simply the reprieve of spending unusually relaxed time out of their cells with peers, making art while also gently goofing around with one another in the ways that children and teens everywhere enjoy frittering away the hours of their youth.

Whatever their motivation, and whatever their mood, they agree that poetry is an important conduit for their hope. They are also unwavering in their belief in reaching out to you with their poems and experiences. They want you to know their struggles and dreams, and they want you to recognize them as human beings, even if the immigration system fails at times to do so.

Take the following poem by Pablito, for example, who fled El Salvador to escape a gang and start a new life in safety and peace.

El futuro

me encuentro en un lugar bajo cuatro paredes,
y cuando miro al cielo veo un presente de angustias,
dolor, rechazos y caídas. Pero muchas veces me
digo a mi mismo: "Si pudiera cambiar mi pasado,
no cambiaría nada porque gracias a los errores
aprendí mucho." Lo importante es seguir adelante
aunque muchas veces andas con una sonrisa fingida,

*pero nadie sabe ni se imagina lo que pasa por
nuestras vidas.*

The Future
I find myself in this place, behind four walls, and
when I look to the skies, I see a present filled with
anguish, agony, rejection, and missteps. But I
often tell myself, "Even if I could change my past, I
wouldn't change a thing because I learned a lot from
the mistakes." The important thing is to keep going,
even if you have to adopt a fake smile, because
no one knows, nor could they imagine, what has
happened in our lives.

Like his peers, Pablito arrived here only after courageously
undertaking an extraordinarily dangerous and lonely trans-
national journey on his own, desperate to try to save and
transform his life after growing up on the streets, orphaned
and surrounded by gangs. His journey to this detention center,
like that of his peers, was an attempted escape from violence,
poverty, and despair. It also has marked and even scarred him,
including his time in isolation.

Still these children persist, even from isolation cells.
They believe in the idea of the United States as "Land of the
Free," and as a nation of immigrants. They also believe in the
so-called "American Dream." Consequently, they often write
and share poems in workshop like the one below. Titled "La
frontera," it was written by Francisco. He is popular for his
interpersonal kindness and patience, evident in his inclina-
tion to transcribe for an illiterate friend, who quietly dictates
his poems aloud to Francisco for transcription. This means,
too, that Francisco often foregoes his chance to write a poem
of his own. He tells me he does not mind because he finds

both activities enjoyable and meaningful. Such is his poet's heart.

His poetic intensity was evident as he wrote "La frontera" one humid morning, the space saturated by the smell of sweat and hormonal teens in tight quarters. His face was stoic beneath his thick head of ink-black hair, and a cherry Dum Dum lollipop dangled from his taut lips, a sugary-sweet delight the children enjoyed in the months before the facility banned me from bringing candy, citing safety concerns.

I remember the focus with which Francisco worked that morning on "La frontera," with both hands on the paper and one toe tapping rapidly on the floor beneath him in its white slipper. His forehead was inches from the table and unwavering, and I sensed powerful verse was being conjured. In general, he is an emotionally daring writer. He is direct and insightful, regularly engaging difficult topics with grit and nuance. That steely diligence stands in contrast to his social self in so far as he would often blush with embarrassment and even get angry at times with his peers when they would press him about his pronounced Indigenous roots.

La frontera
un lugar a que todo el mundo vamos
al tener un sueño
y ver a mi familia feliz
pero no nos dejan llegar a la frontera
por ser de otro país
y me pregunto por qué
si todos somos seres humanos
somos los mismos
no tenemos papeles
porque estamos en el mismo mundo
tenemos sentimientos iguales

el color de piel es diferente
pero eso no quiere decir que no somos iguales
es que en este país en mi país
hay mucha gente racista
el ser blanco, el ser negro
no quiere decir
que no somos iguales
somos todos iguales
tenemos la misma mente
la misma meta
el caminar días por el desierto
al emigrar nos agarra

The Border
a place the whole world goes
when we dream
and want to see our families happy
but they don't let us reach the border
because we're from other countries
and I ask myself why
if we're all human beings
if we're all the same
don't we have papers too
because we're all in the same world
have the same feelings
though our skin colors may differ
but that doesn't mean we're not the same
it means that in this country in my country
there are lots of racists
to be white, to be black
doesn't mean we are
unequal
we're equal

we have the same thoughts
the same goal
to walk for days across the desert
called to immigrate

With the dream of America in their hearts, envisioning safe and healthy futures here, these children have trekked north by foot, by hitchhiking, by bus, and by train, using any means available to them to reach the Mexico-US border. Once arriving there, they still had to dare to try to cross that perilous threshold. It involved a desert that has claimed the lives of more than 10,000 migrants since 1998, according to the US Border Patrol itself.[4]

Besides facing the dangerous conditions, many of the poets in workshop had also been abandoned in their journeys through that desert by their adult companions. These children revealed such trauma by repeatedly writing and speaking in strained voices of surviving scorching days, cold nights, and venomous snakes, of being lost in a vast and desolate expanse by finding and eating raw cactus for nourishment and hydration. Hence their writing would frequently broach experiences of suffering from heat stroke, delirium, exhaustion, and suicidal thoughts in the desert.

Nevertheless, they survived. They persisted in inching their way northward into the contiguous forty-eight states of the United States, only to be found and summarily swept up by US Border Patrol and US Immigration and Customs Enforcement (ICE) agents, often after little more than the briefest glimpse of the country. Consequently, most of the children in this book have known little of the United States, but its carceral system. In other words, they know us only at our most rigid and punishing. And their suffering is as immense as it is deep.

Thus, however much the children may hope in and beyond workshop of better lives, they are haunted by death and despair. Ezequiel, a chubby and good-natured fifteen-year-old father of a baby daughter, explains as much in his poem "El casamiento."

El casamiento

Ayer en mi celda me
dijo mi compañero, mira
¿quieres casarte con la vida
para siempre? Y yo le
contesté ¿para qué
casarme con la vida
si no puedo divorciarme
de la muerte?

Marriage

Yesterday in my cell
my pal asked, Man,
don't you want to marry life
forever? And I
answered, Why
marry life
if I can't divorce
death?

Fortunately, most undocumented, unaccompanied children are not detained under such restrictive conditions. In fact, maximum-security child detainees comprise less than 1 percent of the 57,496 unaccompanied minors that were apprehended along the southern border of the United States in fiscal year 2014, for example.[5] But there is a predilection in federal immigration policy to punish them with incarceration, and often in private detention centers. In 2019, at the height of the carceral policies of the Trump administration on immigration, we saw an annual total of 69,550 children spending time in federal custody, including infants and toddlers. The two largest private prison companies in the United States, the GEO Group and CoreCivic, collectively made more than $1.25 billion in revenue from ICE contracts alone that fiscal year.[6]

During the subsequent Biden administration the trend continued.[7] For example, we witnessed an alarming increase in the use of private immigration detention centers, such that a whopping 90 percent of people in ICE custody were being held in private facilities.[8] And those private facilities continued to rake in billions of taxpayer dollars annually.[9] Additionally, from the start of his presidency until the end of September of 2024, meaning days before the presidential election on November 5, we saw an astounding spike of 140 percent in the number of people incarcerated daily in immigration detention.[10]

The children wish to join you in freedom and go to school, learn English, make good friends, find jobs, and play on local youth sports teams. They wish to pursue dreams of becoming mechanics, lawyers, rappers, doctors, chefs, professional soccer players, and more. In short, they wish to live like most teens in safe, stable, and healthy living environments.

Time and again the children have attested to that in workshop through poetry. However much they would write or speak about grisly violence, brutal heartbreak, agonizing isolation, and severe deprivation, they also managed to create poems and conversations about beautifully imagined futures filled with goodness, joy, fulfillment, hope, and peace.

A very young teen named Gael encapsulated this succinctly in the following poem, titled "Tener un sueño" ("To Have a

Dream"). It was written one muggy, late summer morning in a workshop organized thematically on the occasion of the anniversary of Dr. Martin Luther King, Jr.'s, famous "I Have a Dream" speech. We read and debated that speech together before writing and sharing poems in response to it. Here is Gael's.

Tener un sueño
Sueño con ser el presidente de mi país
Sueño con descubrir un mundo donde no importe
nada más que solo lo que llevas dentro de ti

To Have a Dream
I dream of being the president of my country
I dream of discovering a world where nothing
would matter more than what you carry within

~~~

CHAPTER 2

Suicide Patrol

Your silence will not protect you.

— AUDRE LORDE

I've been running late all morning since my dawn struggle to get my two young sons washed, fed, dressed in winter layers, and to school amidst this snowstorm. Now I'm running late to teach. I have to be in class in fifteen minutes, and I'm not even in the building yet, let alone through the tedious security screening. Snowy roads slog my commute, grinding it to a tense creep on the highway. But now I can speed: on foot, through the long parking lot where I'd wedged my car into a far corner. I slide and skid my way through dirty slush in polished black dress boots, clutching a bundle of books under one arm and a bag of candy for my students under the other.

Huffing behind the thick scarf over my mouth and nose, and sweating under my jacket and sweater, I can feel my laced-up dress boots soaked through to my woolen socks. It's no small relief when I reach the cleared front of the main building with its blacked-out doors and windows. I mash the intercom button with a gloved thumb and announce my name and purpose, eager to reach my students.

"Seth Michelson, to run poetry workshops."

"Okay," crackles a disembodied voice, and I'm buzzed in.

Once inside the small, square vestibule, I start to peel off layers—gloves, jacket, scarf, knitted cap, belt, shoes—knowing this journey begins for me each morning here the way most people begin the process of boarding an airplane: undressing under watchful eyes. I lay my belongings on a long table, including my ID and wristwatch, and then I walk through a metal detector, twice.

"Just to be sure," says a friendly, young guard, telling me with a smile that the beep has been malfunctioning.

With a nod I collect my things, put my belt and watch back on, and progress to the lone window to the guard booth at the entrance to the building's interior. From beneath its square of opaque, one-way glass, a metal drawer shoots out at me and pops open like a hippo demanding food. I drop in my Virginia driver's license, and the box closes and recedes back into the wall.

After a protracted instant, the box shoots out again, returning my license, and a tinny female voice crackles "I'll buzz you in" through a speaker.

I move three steps to my right and wait for a thick metal door to swing open towards me mechanically.

The friendly guard from before indicates that I can pass through it, and he joins me in the tiny, windowless space between two doors. The one behind us bangs closed, and for a moment we're trapped in here together, waiting, waiting, for the next mechanical door to clang open a few feet in front of us.

After a brisk walk down a long hall and then gaining permission to pass through yet another door, I'm entering Cellblock B. The clock hits 8:15 a.m. Time for class to begin. I just made it, even if more disheveled and sweaty than I'd wish.

"*Buen día,*" I say, taking a deep breath to steady myself for the coming experience.

The students sit in groups of four at round metal tables with metal stools. The tables and stools are bolted down to the concrete floor. They're all Spanish-speaking young teens, and boys and girls are intermingled by institutional design that considers their respective countries of origin, migration histories, and psychological needs.

"I'm happy to be with you again," I continue, a warm smile in my voice for each of them.

I look into their faces, trying to discern how each child is doing today. I know it's hard for them to be here. I know their very presence is remarkable.

So here I stand this morning among them in the improvised space for our poetry workshop. It's the central area of the children's cellblock, ringed by the isolation cells that are their homes. Our space is roughly the size of a high school classroom, and it's just as bright with fluorescent light, though here officers, not teachers, circulate amidst the affixed metal tables and stools. Still other officers simultaneously monitor us remotely, using cameras positioned about the room. We are in fact everywhere observed and recorded, which certainly makes it a challenging space in which to write freely. But it's the best we can hope for, and frankly I'm still amazed I've even been allowed in here to do this.

There is little knowledge of this facility outside of ICE and immigration circles. Most of the local residents don't even know it's here, ensconced as it is within a stretch of law enforcement facilities including a regional men's jail and a county juvenile detention center.

My access is unprecedented, and it's necessary because we in the United States need to hear from these children. In discussions of US immigration policies, we often talk about them and for them, but we rarely hear from them themselves. And from my first meeting in here with the children, I knew they had much to add. They had much they wanted to say. They simply needed the forum to express it.

This morning, I begin with my standard opening question: does anyone have anything they'd like to share? Maybe something they've written since our last meeting? Something they've revised? Something they regret not sharing in past workshops?

I remind them that we welcome anything and everything they've composed, regardless of genre, theme, or date, and whether written on paper or in their head. The latter is an especially important reminder in here, where the children not only can lack access to writing materials, but also are often illiterate or barely literate.

So, I remind them frequently, too, that literacy matters little for poetry. I tell them literacy is a mark of educational privilege, not a sign of artistic ability. To reiterate this playfully, I often tell them, "De poeta y loco todos tenemos un poco," which roughly translates to "there's a bit of a poet and a crazy person inside each of us." The aphorism always relaxes them, bringing out smiles and easing nerves enough to evoke writing.

With an eye always on community-building, I regularly remind them, too, that this isn't school; it's a free and open forum for artistic exchange. We are a collective of poets, not "inmates" or "illegals," and we want to write and share with clarity, honesty, and courage. I tell them here is where to cherish and fight for their dreams. I tell them I hope that the workshop will lessen their loneliness and anguish, even if only the tiniest bit, and even if only for the duration of our brief time together each meeting. Though, who knows, it might just create connections that transcend this limited, weekly contact.

At this point, with an open call for contributions hanging in the air above our heads, a brave hand or two will typically shoot up. This morning, to my delight and surprise, the hand that shoots up belongs to Carlitos.

He's one of the youngest children in here, an almost prepubescent thirteen. He has the narrow shoulders of a little boy. His body is slender, and his voice is soft and quiet. He prefers listening to speaking, especially around the older, huskier teens with tattooed hands and faces.

So, I'm delighted he wants to share this morning. We always love to hear from him, however rare the occasion. And what he delivers to us this morning is a display of wisdom well beyond his years.

He speaks a text composed by memory. It's an ode to his deceased mother, the only family member he's ever known. Already his peers are nodding along; too many of them, too, have lost their parents or were orphaned at birth or at a young age.

Carlitos mourns his mother often in workshop, but today is different. For the first time he reveals that she threw him out of their home in Guatemala City when she discovered he had become gang affiliated. Again, his peers in the detention center nod. This, too, is a familiar story in here. More broadly, it's moments in workshop like this that bind the children, who find connection in hearing others' struggles with similar experiences, including losing loved ones to street violence and migrating to escape gang life.

In Carlitos's case, he explains his mother was pulling night shifts, almost making ends meet. He was out huffing paint fumes, tagging walls, and getting arrested, which is how she discovered his miscreance.

She was furious, threw him out, and so he lived on the street, with his *carnales*, or homies. He'd expected her to calm down and welcome him home, but she was killed before that invitation ever came.

And he confesses to us with no small shame that while living on the streets and waiting to be invited home, he'd curse his mom to his *carnales*. Enraged by her decision, his outbursts of angry words covering his sense of helplessness, despair, and hurt.

Halfway through his story, the rage subsides. It transforms into a complex understanding of his mom's strength. He says he realized it was love: she'd thrown him out because she loved him, because she wanted him safe and healthy.

He says he'll never forgive himself for cursing her, never forgive himself for all the pain he caused her. He says he'll never forgive himself for that night when she was kicking him out and all he did was offer a dismissive wave of his hand over his shoulder as he walked out of her life, leaving her in tears in the doorway to the small apartment with the sofa bed they'd shared since his birth.

When she died, he decided to migrate, to honor her memory by saving his own life. He knew she'd always wanted him to leave the gang, rise from poverty, make a good and honorable life for himself.

He was trying. And here he was, six months later, singing out his love for her, and hers for him. It was a painful, soulful song. He was extolling her from a detention center for unaccompanied children, one more orphan among so many others. And with that song, he was planting seeds of compassion in the hearts of his peers. His song was magical: it was altering the ambience of this grisly place for the children in workshop. It was momentarily enlivening and uplifting their spirits. It was a gift, reminding these forlorn children of love's power to sustain them, even burdened as they each were with their respective histories of harsh poverty, pain, abuse, neglect, and terror.

If Carlitos was doing all of this from life in an isolation cell, just think of how he'd flourish in a good public school. Think how he'd thrive with a safe home, with nutritious meals, and with a network of healthy friends. Like every child in here, like any teen, he is full of potential; he is capable of amazing things. Carlitos has trekked alone across multiple nations with almost no money. How many of us could have done that at thirteen?

After finishing his performance, he sits back down on his cold, metal stool and stares at his shoes. Like most writers, he's unsure how the public will react to his new piece. He feels vulnerable, exposed. It's exacerbated by our initial reaction: we sit briefly in stunned silence around him, rocked by the gravitas of his work.

And then the group erupts in applause. Children whoop and shout out praise to him. And I wish I could hug him, knowing he needs the tenderness. But I can't. The institution prohibits touching due to child rape laws, which I understand. Still, it's another missed opportunity, however miniscule, for loving, supportive connection.

Plus, I know Carlitos feels embraced by the group: it's in their applause, their shouted compliments, their inspired faces. His nearest neighbor, Samuel, is so moved that he has leaned over on his stool and is giving Carlitos a kind of half-hug-and-handshake-and-fist-bump. I've come to recognize this gesture, in here among these stoic teen boys, is almost like an expression of gushing love.

I add to the celebration by passing out candy to everyone, beginning with Carlitos. Today I have Sour Patch Kids®, my son Ilan's suggestion. I tell the children he wanted them to try it because it's his favorite. The talk turns to rankings of colors and flavors, and how the candy is so sour it puckers their mouths, tingles their lips.

As they chew and schmooze, I gently turn the talk back to Carlitos's work. I ask them to respond to it not only with broad compliments, which are great and welcome, but also with specificity, honesty, and precision. I explain that doing so shows respect for the author, to whom the composition is so important, and who is so important to us as a member of our poetry group.

They begin by praising Carlitos's courage in confronting those painful feelings, especially in here. They also praise his love for his mother, and hers for him. Several add that they, too, are migrating to honor deceased parents or deceased friends who were like family. Still another child, orphaned at birth, mentions how lucky Carlitos was to have even known his mother.

They also take some time to discuss the support that gangs can offer children. They say the gang is sometimes the only support you can turn to. They say gangs can play the role of an absent family. One boy chimes in that the police in his city in Honduras kill street kids with impunity, something that the gang protected him against; where would he be without them? Another boy adds that if you don't join the gang in his town in El Salvador, its members will try to hurt or even kill you—that is if the other gangs in the area don't get to you first.

Adding to the complexity of our conversation, a young Mexican boy intimates that he fled a cartel in Michoacán when they killed his friend. He feared he'd either be next or he'd be asked to kill for them as a kind of initiation. Both options terrified him, and he ran, stopping only when he was nabbed by US Border Patrol agents in a desert. He didn't even know he was in the United States.

From such conversation, the children now feel more bonded, and this began with Carlitos's narrative. Through the workshop he and the others are forging new ways to connect and to be together, transforming a hostile space into a nourishing one, even if only temporarily. They are building an alternative community within a community. They are creating a space for tenderness, compassion, and self-expression within a state-sponsored cellblock, wherein they're most often commanded about in strict orders to be obeyed in silence.

Against the existentially crippling violence of enforced silence, Carlitos has spoken. After hearing his beautiful piece, many other children want to share work too. We hear a stream of poems, stories, rap lyrics, reflections on detention, and memories of early childhood long before migration. And now we're warmed up to resume the individual task of writing.

To that end I've brought in some poetry to celebrate the self, especially selves in crisis. That might seem too on the nose, but it isn't. These children struggle by the hour to stay alive day after punishing day. That's not hyperbole. A child attended workshop in this very space last week with his wrists heavily bandaged in white gauze because he'd attempted to slit them in his cell.

This morning I've brought in two sample poems to be read aloud by volunteers. I translated them late last night after putting my sons to bed and grading essays by my university students.

The poems are "Tarantulas on the Lifebuoy," by Thomas Lux, and "But What Can You Teach My Daughter," by Audre Lorde. We hear and discuss them in detail. The children are fantastic, as usual. They're deep and sensitive thinkers who love to lose themselves in good writing and good conversation. It breaks my heart to think of all they're denied by being locked away in here.

In particular, they like Lux's deep benevolence for all living creatures in their struggles to endure. And they like Lorde's fierce defense of who she is, and her defense of her child, despite the risks intrinsic to such defenses. I tell the children they're as good at reading literature as any student I've ever worked with, including students at some of the most prestigious universities in the world. In reply, they laugh at me, and Jesús offers a blushing "*No mames güey*" that seems to sum up their collective feeling of disbelief.

But I insist it's true. I do it quickly, not wanting to protest too much. And then I explain our writing goal this morning: write an exploration of self. I mention they're welcome to react to Lux and/or Lorde or set off utterly on their own.

"Now get to work," I add with a smile.

The room goes quiet. The children are thinking.

It's the calm before the storm, or the storm in the head before the storm on paper. And then suddenly everyone is writing. Most work individually, though the illiterate children work in hurried whispers with a partner as scribe. The feel of the room is transformed by the explosion of creative energy. This is the cellblock morphed into an art studio, a vibrant space for creation.

I stroll among the children, watching them etch their explorations of self into their journals in thin, sporadic black ink, a consequence of the tiny, rubber pens provided us by the detention center, the only writing instruments we're permitted to use. Every so often, a letter or even a word is traced on the page, but no ink leaves the pen, leaving the entries with gaps, with ghostly blanks, with defiant erasures in the stories they're struggling to tell, as if all cannot be revealed.

The only noise in the room is the whisper of those pens on paper, and of a few quiet conversations unspooling here and there between our illiterate writers and their scribes, who forgo writing for now in order to help a friend.

A few minutes later, we reconvene. Each child readies himself to share the fruits of their labor. And what ensues is not a poetry reading as much as the emergence of a new constellation in the night sky, with each child's voice a glittering star in it, beautiful in itself and breathtaking in combination.

And what strikes me most about it is a simple thought, one so simple it almost doesn't merit mention: that these writers are children. But it *does* need mention. It's a fact so often overlooked that we can label these children, so full of potential, as dangerous criminals and lock them away in isolation cells to wither.

These are children. They're children in cages. They're children we're punishing for being developmentally typical of their age. They're young teens who've been caged precisely for trying to move from early childhood to the world of adults, which is what they should be doing. In their nascent autonomy, they each made a terribly difficult decision: to migrate to save their lives. They've prioritized hard work, self-discipline, and self-sacrifice in an attempt to effectuate a better future for themselves and for others. Isn't that what we adults so often wish to teach teens to do?

In that context, our cruelty towards them in their youthful striving feels awfully poignant to me this morning as I listen to their new writing. Their texts, one after another, brim with the innocence, juvenescence, and hope of most any teen.

Take, for instance, as a random sample, the four poems below, read aloud just now by the boys at the table nearest me. It is but one table in one cellblock here, which is but one detention center among the roughly 270 spanning our nation.

These poems could have come from four teens at almost any table in almost any school in almost any country. In other words, these are simply the voices of children.

Soy Geraldo

Soy Geraldo. Soy hiperactivo.
Me gusta andar chingando.
Si no, uno está aburrido todo el tiempo.

Ando para arriba y para abajo.
Quiero salir
para ir a la playa.
En Guatemala hay unas
muy buenas y lindas
y unas malas
con basura en la orilla.
Me gusta nadar
y jugar en las olas.
También me gusta pescar
y comer el pescado
y los cangrejos azules.

I'm Geraldo
I'm Geraldo. I'm hyperactive.
I like to goof around.
If not, it's boring all the time.
So I bounce up and down.
I want to leave here
and go to the beach.
In Guatemala, there are
many good and pretty ones,
and many ugly ones
with trash on their shore.
I like to swim
and play in the waves.
I like to fish
and eat my catch,
especially blue crabs.

Soy Edgar
Soy Edgar. Soy de El Salvador.
Y a mí me gusta montar las motos

y hacer carreras.
Quiero ser ingeniero
para diseñar edificios.
Voy a diseñar
mi propia casa.
Tendrá una piscina
y disco
para tener fiestas
todos los días.

I'm Edgar

I'm Edgar. I'm from El Salvador.
And I like to ride
and race motorcycles.
I want to be an engineer
and design buildings.
I'm going to design
my own house.
It will have a pool
and a disco
for having parties
every day.

Soy Omar

Soy Omar. Soy de Honduras
y quiero quedarme aquí.
Quiero trabajar
y hacer feria.
Quiero ser mecánico de autos.
Trabajaría con cualquier auto.
El auto de mis sueños
es un Mustang blanco
con negro convertible.

I'm Omar
I'm Omar. I'm from Honduras
and I want to stay here.
I want to work
and make money.
I want to be an auto mechanic.
I'd work on any car that comes in.
My dream car
is a white Mustang
with a black convertible roof.

Soy Emilio
Soy Emilio. Soy de Guatemala,
tierra de floración y belleza.
Me gusta escuchar música,
dibujar y pintar.
También me gusta el fútbol.

I'm Emilio
I'm Emilio. I'm from Guatemala,
land of flowers and beauty.
I like to listen to music,
draw and paint.
I like soccer too.

Together these poems could comprise a composite portrait
of any random group of teens. You could find these four chil-
dren, or children like them, in most any school, in most any
park, in most any mall, in most any church, and on most any
youth sports team in your town.

CHAPTER 3

~~~~~

Looking for Light

Solidarity involves commitment, and work,
as well as the recognition that even if we do not have
the same feelings, or the same lives, or the same bodies,
we do live on common ground.

— SARA AHMED

How unjustly we judge the lives of others. That's what I keep thinking this frigid December morning.

It's 2019, and I'm in Matamoros, Mexico, a border city that abuts Brownsville, Texas, in the United States. I'm trying to better understand how people are arriving in US immigration detention centers, and with such harrowing personal stories. So, I'm here in the international refugee camp. I am also here at the request of a binational human rights group from Mexico and the United States who know of my work as scholar and poet. They have facilitated my safety. They want me to witness this place and speak of it.

This was the first refugee camp to emerge along the Mexico-US border during the Trump administration. It is also the largest, with its surging population having ballooned in roughly ten months from a few hundred people milling about two different border crossing points to more than 3,500 people now concentrated by the main port of entry to the United States.

That population surge is due directly to President Trump's implementation this past January of a new federal policy known as the Migrant Protection Protocols (MPP).[1] Worse, amidst those swelling numbers of people are swelling numbers of reports of violence among and against them. This includes widespread reports of rampant human rights abuses and crimes such as robberies, assaults, rapes, extortion, kidnappings, and disappeared people.[2]

As aforementioned, this treacherous bottleneck of migrating people is a direct consequence of US policy and the Mexican government's capitulation to it. More specifically, it began in April 2018, when President Trump mandated his version of a "metering" or "queue management" program for people seeking asylum across the southern border of the United States. Previously, anyone arriving at a US border could, by law, request asylum. As of April 2018, the US government was allowing only a few people to do so per day, thereby metering the flow of asylum-seekers into the United States. In fact, that flow was so restricted at times as to stop completely, with no one being allowed to cross, sometimes for days. Meanwhile, the asylum-seekers had to wait in Mexico, a country often foreign, unwelcoming, and violent to them.[3]

Moreover, their wait could last for weeks or even months. It was as exhausting and dangerous as it was baffling and inscrutable. Few people could discern the process by which the names were being chosen for the opportunity to cross the border during metering, nor could anyone anticipate any type of timeframe for being called. In the face of an indefinite wait like this in a dangerous city without adequate safety, money, food, or shelter, some people opted to try to cross the border between ports of entry. This meant daring to trek into deadly desert often by night and, preferably, on one with no moon for added invisibility, or daring to swim a deadly river, again often by night and again, preferably, without even moonlight. Still others abandoned their quests for asylum entirely, and their numbers and fates remain largely unknown. However, many other people did choose to remain here, beside the port of entry, in this unsafe refugee camp, painfully hunkering down, crossing their fingers, and waiting for their lucky day to be called—maybe.

Thus the Matamoros refugee camp was born in Mexico of US policy. And under the US policy of MPP, the camp's population exploded. It would take me some time to understand how that policy impacted what I was seeing, but what I grasped immediately was the cynicism of the name *Migrant Protection Protocols*. MPP was in no way intended to *protect* migrating people; rather, it trapped them here indefinitely in dangerous and desperate conditions.

This morning trapped people were everywhere starving and freezing. A freakish cold spell had overcome the city, plunging temperatures into the low thirties. Few in the camp were ready for it. For months there hadn't been enough food, shelter, medicine, or clean water, let alone reserves of winter gloves, pants, socks, hats, and coats.

Consequently, as I wind my way through the expanse of cheap, flimsy tents that form this sprawling camp, I can't help but wonder what's worse here, the hunger or the cold?

Because on winter days like today, the cold bites your face. It freezes your toes and fingers. I can only imagine what it must be like to wake here, on frozen ground, in thin clothes, inside a rickety tent being slapped and whipped by icy wind. And then to know that that same tent is the warmest, safest place to spend your day, before night falls and the temperature drops, and you lie down on the frozen ground to try again to sleep.

But the belly, too, has its pains. On most days, the only meal here is a free lunch from a US church group. But they can't always make the journey. It's complicated and costly, and the church members are all volunteers. And even when they do make their way here, there's never enough food. There are simply too many mouths to feed. Thousands too many. Thus, the primary modes of eating involve scavenging, though there's also begging, bartering, foraging, and hustling for precarious day labor, often at great risk of physical abuse.

So it's hard to tell whether the people trapped here are suffering more from cold or hunger. What's certain, though, is that suffering is everywhere, and that this massive camp wouldn't exist without US policies such as metering.

Adding to the ubiquitous anxiety here, there's a dispiriting rumor cutting through the camp this morning like the icy wind: the US church group won't be coming, their van broke down in Texas. If true, then hundreds of people here will forfeit the only meal they might have received. Hundreds of people will be left to gnaw their tongues and fill their bellies with water while scrounging the camp for scraps of food, which far too often are nonexistent.

Meanwhile, to fight the cold, to lift the battered spirit, people make small fires beside their tents. It's part physical necessity, part coping mechanism. Over the flames they'll warm their hands and faces, dry wet clothes, and boil water from the Río Grande to clean it. And if lucky enough to have friends here, this is also where they'll gather and chat, the fire dancing in their pupils. And if luckier still, they'll have something to cook, and this is where they'll perform that hallowed feat.

For the kindling and firewood, the refugees have been clear-cutting the scrub brush that forms the eastern and southern borders of the camp. It's small-scale deforestation, and the city of Matamoros has begun to take notice. Government officials and locals alike have started to complain about it, adding to the tensions here. There is real, entrenched resentment between the city and its captives, who, again, are only amassed like this because of US policy. Consequently, there is also real, entrenched resentment of the United States.

Moreover, the anti-migrant resentment here among Matamorenses is growing louder and angrier by the day. I hear it regularly. Many local people have spoken to me with open disdain for their filthy camp and for the refugees themselves.

Among these Matamorenses' more reasonable complaints, the locals grumble about the fundamental unfairness in refugees getting city resources that they themselves need. This includes such basic human necessities as food, water, and clothing, and it's hard to find fault with the logic behind such griping. The impoverished locals here, who are many, have multiple serious needs. I myself see it each day as I walk the streets of this beautiful if at times decrepit city.

Time and again I meet people begging for change. Still others tell me of their daily hardships, which include hunger, unemployment, health woes, and homelessness. More broadly still, I've been told of large-scale food shortages, power outages, and sewage issues. Certainly the local public en masse could use more support, or a better distribution of resources, especially among the most impoverished people in this city.

But the locals' claims of the luxury of life in the camp are also exaggerated, born of intended demonization. They speak as if the refugees were being showered in abundant resources. They'd lead you to believe the refugees live cushy lives in a curated community, wherein they eat extravagant, healthy meals, wear warm clothes, and sleep in lavish accommodations. All this while sapping light, wealth, and water from hardworking Matamorenses.

In reality, though, the refugees are threadbare, hungry, and cold. There is never enough food. There are never enough tents. There are never enough coats. There aren't enough toilets. There aren't umbrellas when it rains or fans for the heat. The refugees are trapped in place, struggling daily to live, exposed to the elements, not to mention the crime and violence, both within and beyond the camp.

Nevertheless, many Matamorenses insist to me that these refugees are coddled. I'm told they're moochers, vagrants, grifters, trash, dimwits, and thieves. I'm told they're making beautiful Matamoros dirty and unsafe. I'm told they're sucking up local resources and bankrupting the city. What's true is that the camp is overspilling with people in need. And what's true is that life for the refugees is dangerous, harsh, and trying. And this is by design.

I say it's by design because it's the foreknown consequence of MPP. Because the policy aims not only to trap these people here cruelly, but also to instrumentalize that display of cruelty as a warning and deterrent against other people who might be contemplating migration to the United States through Mexico.

That said, the most tenable complaint by locals about the refugee camp is not about the relativity of poverty or the personal character of refugees. Instead, it's geopolitical. It's the local indictment by Matamorenses of the arrogance of US policy. They see the United States as intruding here, into their city, their country, and in a way that can't be anything but unhelpful and frustrating. This is why they angrily ask me variations of the question: "Why does your country hold its refugees here, expecting us to take care of them for you?" And I have no good answer. They're right: we've intentionally created refugee camps in Mexico because our president demanded it and Mexican officials obliged.

The refugees have a different take on things. However diverse their complaints about life here, they tend to focus on one thing: the arduousness of their lived experience in this camp in Matamoros.

To wit, many refugees tell me that, yes, they're trapped here in the camp by US policy, but Mexico doesn't take care of them either, whatever the nation may claim. The refugees say that, to the contrary, they're badly mistreated by many locals. The refugees say they're desperate to leave this rotten camp and resume their journeys to the States, but they're prohibited from doing so by the United States and its immigration policies like MPP, which is a kind of invisible cage for them here with bars forged by US legislation.

It might help to take a moment, then, to review how MPP works on the ground, in the lives of these refugees. Perhaps more well known by its colloquial moniker, "Remain in Mexico," MPP is a federal policy overseen by DHS. Most typically it is enforced at the border by US Customs and Border Patrol (CBP). MPP applies to all non-Mexican refugees who have reached the US border by traveling through Mexico, and who request asylum in the United States. According to DHS itself, such refugees must present themselves at a US port of entry, or between US ports of entry, to a US federal agent, who is typically from CBP. When that refugee makes the asylum request of the CBP agent, it triggers MPP. Following MPP protocol, the agent responds to such requests for asylum by registering the refugee's personal details and assigning them a Notice to Appear (NTA) in a US federal immigration court. The agent then initiates the return of the refugee to Mexico, where they must remain until the court date indicated on their NTA, which can be months away. Hence the huddled masses of refugees popping up in camps along Mexico's northern border, including the roughly 3,500 people trapped here in Matamoros.

More ominously, very few, if any, of these refugees are aware of the grim statistics that await them in MPP cases. For example, according to DHS, from MPP's inception in January of 2019 to October of 2020, meaning from President Trump's implementation of the program until his final days in office before losing the presidential election to Joe Biden on November 3, only 43,820 MPP cases were successfully completed in US courts.[4]

Here the phrase *successfully completed* does not mean the refugee won their asylum case. Rather, it simply means that the refugee was able to properly and completely fill out their paperwork, submit it to the courts, have it accepted by the courts as complete, and have it reviewed by a judge, regardless of outcome. Compare that figure to CBP's self-reported registration of more than 1,794,846 "enforcement actions" with undocumented people during 2019 and 2020.[5]

In part, the number of "successfully completed" cases is proportionally tiny due to the relative inability of people in refugee camps to complete and file their paperwork. The very conditions of their forced migration and status as inhabitants of refugee camps makes the process difficult for them. First, the camps are insecure, and resources are scarce. This includes a lack of credible information about the process and assistance with pursuing it. Additionally, the paperwork is in English, and it is intricate. Few people in the camps have the language, education, and legal training to complete the paperwork properly on their own. Moreover, they most often lack the resources to retain an attorney, even if one were available to them. Thus, they often err in filling out and filing their forms, and/or they fail to see their paperwork through to completion in the courts. This is often due to the instability and insecurity of their lives in refugee camps in Mexico and the variability of the dates, times, and locations of their court proceedings, if any.

Worse still, of those 43,820 properly filed cases, only 523 succeeded in court[6]. That means that after struggling to reach the Mexico-US border, presenting themselves to CBP, receiving an NTA, being returned to Mexico (and perhaps to somewhere in Mexico far from their original point of entry into the United States). All while awaiting their US court date stuck in a Mexican refugee camp, somehow filing their paperwork properly, and succeeding in court. Only 523 of those 43,820 people were granted permission to stay in the United States, at which point they can merely *begin* to pursue their asylum claims.[7]

That is to say that a refugee in MPP has roughly a 1 percent chance of being granted permission to stay in the US and begin to seek asylum, which is in itself an arduous, expensive process typically lasting about two years. Moreover, the outcome of that two-year process is far from certain, meaning the refugee could still lose their case and be denied asylum, resulting in their deportation from the United States.

Meanwhile, the refugees in Mexican refugee camps wait on a prayer for the outside chance to appear in US court on the date indicated on their NTAs. And while waiting, they endure the terrible dangers of life in the camp, and of life beyond it. Here in Matamoros, for example, the refugees frequently relate to me many of these dangers, most of which emerge from their attempts simply to subsist. For instance, they regularly lament the lack of opportunity here for them to find work. They tell me of being desperate to find jobs, any jobs, so as to be able to buy food and find safer shelter than the camp while awaiting their NTA date. But, in general, the Matamorenses won't hire them, even for day labor. Thus, many people languish in the camp, hungry, vulnerable, and afraid.

On the rare occasions when a refugee does find work in Matamoros, it usually ends badly. They are frequently shorted on pay or not paid at all, and there's no safe recourse for that. If they complain, they're run off by violence, the threat of violence, or the threat of having the police called on them, which never ends well for the refugee. One frazzled Guatemalan woman in her early thirties tells me how just yesterday morning she was thrilled to find work sweeping and mopping a store's floors before it opened, only to finish proudly and be run off unpaid by the shop owner. He threatened to beat her with the very broom he'd had her use to sweep. Her hands tremble with indignation as she tells me this. She says she's hungrier than ever, but too scared and distrusting to try again right now to find work.

A nearby Honduran father with a big, bushy mustache and a tween daughter at his side overhears us. He jumps into our conversation, wanting to add his story and commiserate. He tells us that to feed his wife, daughter, and baby son, he'd spent a long and arduous afternoon loading bags of cement onto truck beds. He says the work was fast-paced and demanding, and he'd been told the pay would accordingly be good. But things ended menacingly, with the final truck loaded and with him being smacked around by the boss and a clutch of his underlings. Some of the underlings waved tools at him threateningly as weapons. He didn't dare stick around to demand his money.

Stories of wage-theft like these circulate in the camp, and their damage runs deep. They're not only disappointing in themselves for the victimized refugee, but they also work as warnings to other refugees: don't even try to seek work. And all of that only intensifies the general sense of despair, disempowerment, and hunger here among the refugees.

More disheartening still, the crimes against refugees are not limited to wage-theft. For example, a petite Mam woman from Guatemala, somewhere in her late forties or early fifties and with wisps of gray hair at her temples, tells me in soft-spoken Spanish (meaning her second language), of being assaulted by a group of local youth. As she tells it, she'd gone out one morning to search for food for her family when she crossed paths with foulmouthed locals. They began slurring her for being Indigenous, and their words stung her, but she was fine until they began to follow her. They pursued her down several streets, shouting, "You don't belong here!" Then they began hurling rocks and garbage at her. Something heavy hit her nape, which still hurts. Something else grazed her head, knocking off her hat, which she abandoned. She just kept hurrying back towards the camp as fast as she could, saying nothing and keeping her head down. "Eventually they must've lost interest," she explains. "I haven't left the camp since."

A Salvadoran man in a cowboy hat offered me a similar story of xenophobic violence. He'd been out searching for a construction site that he'd heard about from a neighbor here, but instead of finding work, he stumbled across a group of teens. They surrounded him and demanded to know where he was from and what he was doing in their neighborhood. Upon hearing his accent and his answer, they began insulting him as a foreigner and leech, and spat on him. Some hit his face. When he turned to run, they began to chase him, shouting insults and threatening to beat him up. He ran for several blocks before they disappeared behind him. "I've never been spit on before," he tells me with shame, "but I'm glad it wasn't worse."

From conversations with many other refugees here, I already understand what *worse* means. It means acts of severe physical violence, including beatings, armed robberies, rape, and kidnappings, often with torture.

For example, yesterday evening while I was preparing the paperwork for a Salvadoran teen mother to cross the border with her toddler for her NTA, she mentioned tangentially that the two of them had been abducted off the street here a couple of weeks ago. She said she'd been out begging for change to buy milk for her child when they were kidnapped and taken to a vacant office or a warehouse. She wasn't sure of the location, she said, because of the stress and terror. What she was sure of, though, is that she was sexually abused by three different men, and with her child right there on the floor beside her.

Another Salvadoran mother, mousy and petite, trusted me with her kidnapping story, too, while we were drawing up her asylum paperwork. She explained that she'd set out one sunny morning here to try to earn some money for food for her hungry family. She'd hoped to find work washing dishes in a restaurant or cleaning the floors of a store or someone's home. Instead, she was kidnapped by a carload of men who drove her to a safehouse, where she feared she'd be raped and killed. Blindfolded, she began to pray the rosary. But these kidnappers weren't rapists or murderers; they were extortionists. They tied her to a chair, slapped her around a bit, and began texting threats to her extended family back in San Salvador. They demanded money in exchange for not killing her. "Thankfully, my uncle paid," she said to me. "That's why I'm alive today."

It's hard to imagine that either of these two kidnappings would've occurred were it not for MPP trapping these two families here. And they're far from being the only refugees to be victims of violent crimes while stuck here in purgatory.

For instance, Susana, a Guatemalan mother of three, tells me a story that similarly haunts me to this day. She says Belén, who'd lived alone in the tent next to hers, has been missing now for two weeks. She'd headed out to search for food one afternoon but never returned. The rumor was she'd been kidnapped and killed by a cartel. Her empty tent still stands in the camp with all of her belongings in it. Susana and her family guard it like a religious relic, hoping for the miraculous return of their friend and neighbor.

Sadly, such disappearances are not unusual here. The telephone poles on the city street that forms the western border of the camp are covered with flyers that broadcast the faces, names, and dates of disappearance of countless people, including children. I meet Roxana, who fears she'll be next.

She's twenty-two, tall, slender, and gentle. She could pass for fourteen. She's also alone here, like Belén had been. This makes her an easy target everywhere she goes, both within and beyond the camp. She can't wait to get out of here. She has to. Her life depends on it.

That's what she tells me, repeatedly. And each time she says it, I'm struck by her intensity. It's in the strength in her voice, and her eyes brim with the same conviction. I also feel it in her body language. All of this I absorb while sitting side by side with her. At her request, we're on the half-crumbled curb of an empty parking lot owned by a cartel. It's where she'd asked to meet me, for safety. Such are the complexities of life here.

And although it's only 8:45 a.m., a long line has already formed a few blocks away for the free lunch that might arrive with the US church group. Like those in line, Roxana is famished, but here she sits, preferring our meeting to any meal.

I offer to meet with her later in the day, after she's eaten, but she emphatically declines, wanting to meet now, here. Her situation is that urgent, that desperate. She's not only enduring the strain of being cold and hungry, but also of living in the camp as a proud and open trans woman.

As we talk, our spindly legs jut out in front of us into an empty parking space. Every so often hers sway, and our bodies touch gently at the knee as if to underscore the importance of human connection.

It's 42 degrees Fahrenheit. Winter wind whips our faces. Roxana has no gloves, no hat, no coat. She's wearing nothing but three long-sleeved T-shirts, and each one is as thread-bare as it is stained at both cuff and collar. I offer her my coat and gloves, to keep for good, but she declines, saying she's fine as is. Every so often between comments, she'll blow into her cupped hands for warmth. And each time, a cloud of vapor forms around her fingers, then dissolves upward into invisibility.

She keeps telling me she can't wait to get out of here. She's desperate to leave the camp, cross the border. She wants to leave Matamoros behind and begin life in the States. "I'll find a way or die trying."

Her voice accumulates force as she continues on, like a locomotive gaining speed. She's now brainstorming her options aloud, for me to hear: wait months for her NTA, swim the Rio Grande at night, trade a sex act with a trucker for a hidden ride in his trailer, forge a passport and papers, cross by daring to hike through deadly desert and mountains, or rush the US border patrol station on foot without papers—dogs and machine guns be damned.

Regardless of how, she has to cross. This much she insists on with clarity. Staring me straight in the eye, she reminds me that her life depends on it. It's her safety. Her well-being. Her future. Her dream. She wants to go to school for fashion, learn English, start a career, fall in love, raise children—she's almost breathless now as she continues to effuse a steady stream of beautiful aspirations. But in the very rush of her words, I can also feel her anxiety, her desperation.

Sensing my growing concern, she swerves into reassurances. She says she's confident she'll realize those dreams. All she needs is the chance. She knows it. She says her confidence is grounded in all that she's already overcome, just to be here.

Her father kicked her permanently out of the family home in San Sula, when she was barely fifteen, for being a trans girl, which he couldn't understand. He'd called her "a plague against God" and "a disgusting sin" before shoving her out the front door for good. She hasn't seen him since.

Worse still, in their final interaction, he hadn't only shouted vile insults at her. He'd also beaten her. He'd in fact slapped her around their living room so violently that she'd ended up with a bloody nose and a fat lip.

Sadder still, that explosion of abuse by her father was nothing new. He'd spent much of their final two years together smacking her around their home while slurring her for being trans. When the door slammed on her that fateful night, it was all over. In a way she was thankful.

She's been on her own ever since, surviving on the streets. At first, she missed her little sister so terribly that it paralyzed her with grief. She felt at times she couldn't even breathe. The two had been that close. So Roxana spent her first weeks alone mostly sobbing. Her sister had been the only one in the world who'd accepted her and who understood her dream of fully transitioning. And now the sisters could no longer see each other.

Depressed and lonely, Roxana wandered homeless through their neighborhood without hope. She felt like its many stray dogs, sleeping on any sun-warmed patch of sidewalk by a church or in any available bushes in the park. Both were prime places for her to avoid beatings by local gangs and police for being a street kid.

Like this she subsisted until a miracle occurred one rainy afternoon: she followed a stray dog through a broken window into the dank basement of an abandoned building. It had no water, heat, or electricity, but it became her refuge, her safe space. Therein she slept, and therein she made money to eat by washing other peoples' dirty clothes.

She did the wash by hand, in a tub of cold water, using a box of powdered soap she'd pinched from a corner store. Day after day, she'd scrub out their stains, returning their lives to a lustrous cleanliness. She says their underwear was always the worst. Still, it was better than being on the streets, begging for change. And who knows how many beatings by gangs and police that blessed basement spared her?

"One night they raped me in driving rain," she says, her strong voice having fallen to a whisper.

"The gangs or the police?" I ask as gently as possible.

"That night, two gang members. I remember just staring up at the moon and waiting for them to finish."

I shudder as the wind picks up. I touch my cheeks; they're freezing.

Being trans in the streets, in this camp, a survivor . . . Roxana can't wait.

"Once I was punched so hard in the face that both my eyes swelled closed," she tells me. She adds,

"I've been strangled unconscious." She goes on,

"One night a guy high on drugs tried to kiss me in an alley. He knifed me when I refused."

"That dawn I decided to immigrate," she adds quickly, pushing up her three right sleeves to show me the scar on her forearm: a broken whorl of jagged skin that looks to me almost like a semicolon. It reminds me of those tattoos people get for suicide awareness, symbolizing the struggle to survive, to fight to live.

No, Roxana can't wait. She needs safety and opportunity. She needs protection in the United States. She's a refugee. She has a right to request it. She qualifies for it. Her immigration process should be efficient and affordable by law.

She says that she'll make it, even if that means crossing without papers and starting life on the streets, living in the shadows. She'll manage, she tells me assuredly. "I've done it before, and in tougher places."

She explains that she craves a community that embraces LGBTQ+ people, one like those she's seen on US TV shows. She loves *RuPaul's Drag Race* and *Queer Eye for the Straight Guy*, but *The L Word* is her favorite.

She can hardly believe the freedom, safety, and acceptance for gay and trans people in the States, at least as seen on TV. And she can't wait to live like them, unafraid and joyful in public and with their partners.

She can't wait to find a job, rent an apartment, sleep indoors in a bed, cook breakfast in a kitchen.

She can't wait to enroll in school, start learning from teachers, do homework, earn a degree.

She can't wait to complete her transition. She tells me she's tired of being caught in between but punished fully.

Again her voice drops to a whisper, but this time it's full of excitement, hope. "I've heard of a gay surgeon in Texas who speaks Spanish. He's sure to help me. All I need to do is get there."

Lord knows she's tried. Repeatedly. Most recently, she crossed somewhere north of Reynosa. It was five or six weeks ago and well past midnight when US border agents plucked her soaking wet and freezing from the Río Grande.

"My mistake was not accounting for the light of the full moon."

Worse, the agents insisted on treating Roxana as a man, even deadnaming her. They also put her in a cell with men, not women. She felt humiliated and unsafe. She couldn't wait to get out of there, no matter where they sent her, even back to Mexico.

Instead they transferred her to a *hielera*, or a freezing-cold holding cell. There, at her insistence, she'd been held with women, which was a relief. But there was no easy camaraderie amongst the captive women and girls. Everyone kept to themselves by necessity, trembling with cold, hunger, and fear.

"When will it end?" she kept thinking. "When will I be released, and where to?"

But her nightmare dragged on.

On her third afternoon in that icy place in the desert, she was called from the cage and marched into a room with a black plastic telephone. It linked her to a prosecutor in Mexico. He immediately began to upbraid her and demand that she "behave."

"Stop pretending to be a woman," he hissed at her. "Stop playing games with the US agents. You're making a fool of yourself, and also of us Mexicans!"

Roxana's ear burned with shame and rage at his words. She couldn't wait to get off the call.

"When he called me a 'stupid faggot,' I hung up on him." Roxana couldn't wait.

Two US agents in green uniforms, angered by her phone etiquette with their Mexican associate, seized her roughly and shoved her back to the holding pen.

"Hours later they returned and grabbed me again without saying a word. They pushed me into a van, and I was driven to the border with several other migrants. There, US agents forced us to walk ourselves back into Mexico, and that's why I'm here."

But Roxana can't wait to get back to the States. She has no family, friends, or money here. She knows neither the city nor the country, and it's not her destination. But her court date on her NTA is still more than two months away.

Meanwhile, she battles through each day here.

"People stalk me. They follow me around the camp and to my tent.

"Twice already I've been beaten.

"The first night they stole my sweater and sneakers."

Roxana can't wait.

"When I try to sleep, they bang on my tent walls. Several times they've even come crashing in."

Roxana can't wait.

"One night while I was washing my hands at the public sink by the porta johns, a man shoved his tongue down my throat and reached into my pants."

Roxana can't wait.

She can't wait for safety.

She can't wait to make a life.

She can't wait for food, a job, the chance to study, start a career.

She wants to design clothes, learn English, go on dates, live her truth in peace. But MPP is thwarting all of that.

"When I go to the bathroom here, they glare at me—men, women, and even children. Their eyes tell me how much they hate me. Why? I'm a kind, generous woman."

Not knowing what to say, I simply hug her. Then we sit in silence on that crumbled curb, my arm around her shoulder.

CHAPTER 4

Dilley

What shall we plant for the future?

— MARILYN CHIN

Seven a.m. Marta was sweating her way through the jungle of southern Chiapas. She was alone, and she was worried. Something was wrong. Even the birdsong sounded ominous.

Her stomach was knotted with fear. Fear buzzed electric in her ears. Her partner, Lisbeth, hadn't met her behind the church at dawn as agreed.

That wasn't like Lisbeth. She was punctual. She kept her word. It was how they'd been together for a year now as a secret couple, despite gay relationships being forbidden in their village and despite Lisbeth being married to Marco for more than a decade.

Two days ago, though, Lisbeth had finally left him, had finally fled his raging fists. With Marta's help she'd escaped deep into the jungle, for peace, safety. They'd prepared a hideaway there for her, a grounds for a new beginning, far from Marco's drunken rampages, far from the hissing insults, the harsh beatings, and the thing she dreaded most: the forced sex, excruciating, furious. The concept of marital rape was unknown to her, foreign to her culture, so she'd close her eyes, pray to die, and weep silently inward.

She wanted to be with Marta, and Marta wanted that too. They'd been friends since childhood and in love for years. But they could never be together, at least not in their village. *A woman needs a man*, the elders constantly preached, as did their respective parents, no matter the black eyes or cracked ribs, the fat lips or broken wrists. Lisbeth's list of injuries was as long as Marco's empty apologies.

So Marta and Lisbeth loved in secret, tenderly, sweetly. And they dreamed of living together one day, openly, free, even if that meant being isolated deep in the jungle. There they'd create a home together, fatten a goat, make *cajeta* and cheese from its milk, and they'd grow a garden flush with maize, squash, and beans. Each sunrise they'd drink coffee together, and they'd fall asleep at night in each other's arms. But for months, whenever Marta would ask Lisbeth when she was thinking of leaving Marco, something dark would drift across her face, and she'd go silent for a solid minute before looking down and whispering as if to no one, "I don't know if it can be done."

Marta understood. It was terrifying even to consider. Both women had heard Marco swear time and again that he'd kill Lisbeth if she ever tried to leave him. Once he'd even forced and locked her outside naked overnight in the rain to punish her for having merely threatened it while he was beating her with a stick.

Marta winced now recalling that memory, Lisbeth's tearful confession of it to her late one night as they lay together naked after loving. So Marta hurried on through the jungle, her sense of desperation surging along with her anxiety.

In her haste, she lost the path. It was so new as to be almost indiscernible. That had been done intentionally. The two women had hewn the route only by foot, and not by machete, hoping to obscure the way, to leave it mostly hidden, for Lisbeth's safety out here in her makeshift sanctuary.

But now it was Marta who'd been confused. She scanned the treetops for guidance. She scrutinized her surroundings, desperate to remember any landmarks. And she studied the ground for footprints, snapped branches, flipped rocks, trampled roots, anything that could potentially indicate the trail, redirect her to Lisbeth.

It worked. A spray of bent grass pointed the way, and Marta followed. She felt a surge of hope and began to imagine herself bumping into Lisbeth at any moment now, around every turn.

She imagined their sudden delight in reconnecting, the soft smiles spreading across their faces, the gentle grace sparkling in Lisbeth's chocolate eyes as the two of them laughed at Marta's needless worry. She could even feel Lisbeth in her arms again, could smell her hair as they lingered in an embrace, two warm bodies in love, fused into a single, red hyacinth.

But those were fantasies. Marta knew it. She scolded herself: *There's no time for dreaming.* Something was wrong. She knew it. She had to find Lisbeth, had to fix whatever it was that was the matter with her this hot, humid morning.

Just when Marta felt she could no longer bear the pace or the worry, she stumbled into a small clearing. She knew she'd made it. Here was Lisbeth's hideout, her safe haven, their future sanctuary as a couple.

But instead of relief, Marta froze with terror. Suddenly she couldn't breathe. For there was Lisbeth, naked and twisted, in a lifeless heap at their home-to-be.

Her face had been split open by a deep machete blow, from the crown of her brow to the bridge of her nose.

Marta saw other slashes too: on Lisbeth's forearms, shoulders, back, throat. And the blood. So much blood. It looked more black than red to her in the morning haze beneath the trees, and it had pooled around Lisbeth's body, turning the fine red dirt to sticky mud.

Marta fell to her knees in it, cradled Lisbeth's head, and wept for all that was lost.

~~~~~~~

Fighting through tears, Marta tells me all this in a small, stuffy interview room in Dilley, Texas. We're inside a double-wide trailer on the grounds of the South Texas Family Residential Center, the largest immigrant detention center in the United States for women and their children, with 2,400 beds.

It's roughly seventy miles south of San Antonio, tucked away in a desolate stretch of desert. It's hard to reach and out of view, keeping its function far from public scrutiny.

Outside the trailer, it's over 100 degrees Fahrenheit. The sun beats down on the metal box we're sitting in. But inside, it's almost chilly, the air-conditioning chirring like an arctic bird.

It's my second stint here as a volunteer, so I knew this morning to dress in layers. Between the parking lot and these interview rooms, the temperature can plummet thirty degrees. So today I'm wearing an undershirt, a white long-sleeved dress shirt, and green cotton slacks with thick socks inside laced-up black boots. I also have a gray sweater at the ready in my briefcase, along with two yellow legal pads, breath mints, and a metal water bottle filled to the brim.

I'm grateful to be allowed to bring the water in. We've long fielded complaints about the water in the facility being dirty, even toxic. And without my breath mints, I'd worry I'd torch a client's face with coffee breath in these small, tight interview rooms.

I'm grateful, too, simply to be here, to be part of this volunteer legal team. I believe wholeheartedly in our mission of ending family detention. And even though I'm no lawyer, they've accepted me, trained me, and sent me in here to help in every way possible. And those ways are many.

This week, we volunteers number a mere eight people. We're the only advocates for the women and children inside this facility, which spans more than fifty acres and boasts more than 600 employees and more than 2,000 people in detention.

I sometimes pause with amazement that ICE has even let us in here to do our humanitarian work. After all, we're adversarial to their very existence. Our aim is to see these refugees freed, woman by woman, and with their children, if any.

To that end, we meet with the women first in groups and then one-on-one. Our goal is to help them to prepare themselves step-by-step for their credible fear interviews (CFIs) with a US Asylum Officer (AO). That AO will either determine the woman to be eligible to pursue asylum in the United States, freeing her from this facility, or initiate her deportation to her country of origin, typically within forty-eight hours. But even in the latter case, we volunteers continue to advocate for the women, explaining to them their right to appeal the AO's decision before a federal immigration judge, if they so wish. At their request, we will even accompany them into that courtroom for emotional support, though we cannot speak in there by legal protocol.

In many ways, this work is part and parcel of my broader commitment to immigration reform. Rooted deeply in childhood experience and cultivated through academic travel and study, it has become a forty-year patchwork of interwoven actions, languages, projects, skills, research, writing, teaching, and experiences. And whatever the undertaking—whether a boisterous poetry workshop with detained teens or a quiet conversation with a rape victim in a refugee camp—I've come to ground my work in practices of empathic listening, and I arrive ready to put myself and my privileges in the service of others however helpful within the framework of their direction and wishes.

Such is the case here in Dilley. The lion's share of my effort ends up devoted to helping the women and their children, if any, to tell their stories of migration and their hopes for the future in their own words. Accordingly, I draw heavily on my skills as a scholar, teacher, and poet. First, I interview the women in Spanish via my project's protocol, listening empathically to all they share. I then guide each woman to focus on strengthening the structure, clarity, pacing, diction, tone, and precision of her personal narrative. Simultaneously, I also share pertinent information about immigration law, policy, and practices, which derives both from my own research and from direct and extensive consultation and training with highly accomplished immigration attorneys.

The goal is to help each mother to leave our one-on-one meetings feeling well-informed, well-prepared, and empowered to convey her personal narrative with truth, eloquence, and power to an AO. It is no small ask as the women and their children are terribly traumatized by the past, which is invariably filled for each of them with poverty, violence, fear, and insecurity. Thus, it is painful for them to recount it, whether to a sympathetic volunteer from my team or to an intimidating US official whom they know will decide nothing less than their very future.

In other words, the process here in Dilley is riddled with holes through which a refugee woman's life could easily slip and disappear. My colleagues and I do our best to redress this, but we are restricted by ICE and by the facility, which limit us to this one trailer on these vast premises. For example, we are not allowed into the cafeteria hall, where we would love to set up a table and explain to women that we are here, offering free services and advocacy for their immediate release. Instead, we must entrust that our presence here spreads by word of mouth among the detained women. Consequently, hundreds of women pass through the facility and are deported without ever knowing that they could have collaborated with an empathic advocate for their release into freedom.

Even still, my fellow volunteers and I remain inundated each day with more clients than we can see. Additionally, we must sometimes confront the agents in power here, albeit politely and selectively. For example, I have had to intervene in CFIs when an AO misunderstands my client and/or her children in perilously crucial ways. Such interruptions run counter to the protocol of the governmental procedure, as well as to the training of my volunteer group. We are especially trepidatious in such instances because the personalities of the AOs can vary quite a bit, and any interruption risks angering the AO in whose hands our client's future so delicately lays.

In one such moment, I was quietly listening to my client, Sandra, explain through sobs her violent extortion by a local gang. A single mother of two young children, she ran a very humble, impromptu tortilla stand on the sidewalk in front of her home in an exceptionally impoverished neighborhood in Guatemala City. There the gang had been demanding a weekly payoff from her, which she had always paid out of fear of their death threats and their acts of violence against her and her young children, including slaps, beatings, destruction of property, strong-arm robbery, the threat of rape, and the threat of child kidnapping.

In economic terms alone, the extortion had wreaked havoc on the family of three. The gang's visits typically left Sandra penniless and forced to beg on the street to try to feed her hungry children. One evening, while out begging like this, she was set upon by the gang. They threatened her, demanded she stop begging, and then followed her home. There they pushed their way inside, beat her, and robbed the house. All the while, they threatened to rape her and kidnap her children. As they left, they also growled that they'd soon return. Later that same night, terrified and desperate to save her children's lives and her own, she fled her home in haste with them in tow, aiming for the United States and carrying only a single plastic bag, filled with her children's clothing.

Unfortunately, the AO did not understand Sandra's story. His confusion hinged on the noun "leche," which denotatively means "milk" in Spanish. However, Sandra was using "leche" as dialectical slang to refer to the extorted money. In his bafflement, the AO asked his remote, Spanish-language interpreter on speakerphone to explain to him what a "milk tax" was. The interpreter said she did not understand, either. That is when I dared to interrupt them and explain the term, believing it crucial to Sandra's claim of credible fear. Had I not done so, what decision might the AO have made for my client and her children, whose very lives hung in the balance?

Speaking of the children incarcerated here, it bears mention, too, that they have been as young as six months old. There are also multiple credible complaints of mothers being denied formula for their babies. Moreover, every detained person is treated adversarially by the state in their immigration proceedings, regardless of age. I have been in CFIs with women and their children where the AO asks a *toddler* a question, noting the child's response and seemingly integrating it into the calculus for determining the credibility of the mother's asylum claim.

This morning, though, my client, Marta, has no children. Marta, who has just withdrawn into private grief. So I simply sit with her in a heavy silence and wait.

I'm in a plastic chair on one side of a metal office desk, and she's in a plastic chair on the other. I lament the distance between us, but it's obligatory by institutional rule. *There's to be no touching of detainees*, and I religiously abide by the mandate. The office desk helps me to prove it to any guard who might pass by our room and peek in through the window in the door.

My job this morning is to prepare Marta to earn her release from here by proving to a US asylum officer that she has a credible fear of returning to her country of origin, Mexico. The interview is scheduled for this afternoon, and I think her case a winning one. That is, if she can share it.

That's no small struggle for traumatized people like Marta. Often the memories come disordered and murky, the mind protecting the person from past violences that exceed their mere facticity. So details might be missing, repressed, partial, or they might return belatedly, after a migrant has told her story to multiple border patrol agents, for example. Or details might remain buried, conspicuously lacking, too agonizing or debilitating to be allowed by the mind to resurface and circulate in active consciousness. And if the traumatized person does recall a violence suffered, it is often too painful to articulate to others. It can feel humiliating and agonizing to confide. On top of that, they often fear they'll be disbelieved if they do speak their truth.

So I sit in labored silence with Marta as she grieves and remembers and recollects and tries to recompose herself for our needed conversation. We've already discussed the process, how in a few hours she'll have to share her story in as much detail as possible with an asylum officer. In a certain sense, it's a cruel and absurd ask: tell this stranger in explicit detail of your greatest suffering. But it's the only way. So I've been rehearsing with Marta how to stay calm, keep events in order, and answer all questions honestly and completely.

I've also been encouraging her to enunciate every word, carefully, cleanly, because the US asylum officer will likely be using an interpreter on speakerphone during the interview, adding a layer of strain to an already painful and awkward conversation by making it choppy, disjointed, and slowed.

Right now, though, Marta can't even speak. She sobs quietly to herself, a world away. I wish I could reach out and hug her. Or at least lay a supportive hand on her shoulder. But, again, I can't: no touching.

Instead I look out through the window in our door and check on our waiting area. I see it's packed already with women and children. I say "waiting area," but it's just the central space of the trailer, wherein we offer a scattering of chairs around a handful of small round tables. Around each, women sit in clusters, chatting, waiting, with children on their laps or at their feet or in chairs beside them. Here and there a lone woman naps or twiddles her thumbs or stares at her feet.

Surrounding that central space are our interview rooms. They line the two long walls of the trailer. And there's an entrance at each end of the trailer, each with a team of guards working from a desk. They monitor all access to the trailer, and all activity herein, aided by cameras on the ceiling.

Seeing we're busy as always, I know that after prepping Marta, I'll get my next client from our ever-growing list. I'll call out her name into the waiting room and smile at the woman who correspondingly rises from her seat. I'll escort her into the interview room, and we'll begin the very process I'm now deep in with Marta.

Alternatively, I might be asked by our staff leader to give a *charla*, or group talk, to ten to twenty incoming women, instead of picking up a new client. It's something I enjoy because it involves orientating the women to our role in here as their free and voluntary advocates. I also enjoy it because I get to welcome the women warmly to the United States, something few to none of them have ever heard, even with all their contact with diverse US officials.

Against that dehumanizing frigidity of our immigration system, my group is trained to practice all kinds of small, interpersonal gestures of hospitality, and it makes a difference. For example, you can clearly see a sense of delighted surprise and ease wash momentarily over the women in a charla when we simply *welcome* them, say we're glad they're here and that we'll fight for them to stay, if that's what they choose.

Infrequently, before delivering a charla or picking up my next client, I might go quickly to the bathroom, or I might devour half a sandwich in three bites while standing at the instant coffee maker in our break room, listening to it spit and gurgle its goodness into a paper cup for me.

But most of the time, I'm with individual women like Marta, who courageously muster their stories, word by agonizing word, in an interview room. And I spend the day moving from one client to the next, avoiding breaks and delays, striving to prime as many women as possible for their interviews with US asylum officers before my team and I have to leave reluctantly for the day. And my team does the same.

Often, too, I prime children, because the moms intend to bring them along to the interview instead of leaving them in the facility's daycare. They tend to want their children always in direct view, if not right with them.

It's understandable, but it's worrisome, too, and for multiple reasons. Chief among them, in our meetings and in the interview with the asylum officer, the children will overhear their mothers telling stories of shocking violence. Granted, those stories likely aren't new to the children's ears, unfortunately. They may have even lived through them themselves and have active memories still haunting them. But to hear them told by their sobbing mothers has to be traumatic, or retraumatizing, for them.

Also problematic, if the children are in the official interview, then the asylum officer might ask them questions. It's a terrifying premise for any child: being asked intense questions by an imperious adult behind an intimidating desk, his face as serious as those in the somber photos of old men hanging on the wall behind him, some in military uniforms. Plus, the answers can be impacting. A child might say something the asylum officer could misconstrue as contradictory to the mother's rendering of the family's past. It could hurt her credibility, destabilize her claim of credible fear, her quest for asylum, leading them to be deported. So I try to prepare the children too. Even ones as young as three have been known to be asked questions by asylum officers, as crazy as that sounds.

Such are the conditions under which my team works in here, and I treat each minute as precious. I don't want to waste time on lunch breaks or bathroom breaks or on the completion of paperwork that I could do later, after hours, in my motel room. My team's days are frenzied and exhausting; we know the stakes are as high for the women as their days are stressful. I'm already a drone, buzzing at their service, a whirling cog in the wild machine of our advocacy. And I'm already wearied, though I've only just flown in yesterday.

It took me two flights and nine hours to reach San Antonio International Airport from my hometown airport in Charlottesville, Virginia. Then I hopped into a rental car for the ninety-minute drive to a cheap motel in Dilley, near the detention center. Along the route, I'd grabbed a week's worth of groceries at a local market, knowing I'd have a mini fridge in my motel room because I'd dropped fifteen extra bucks per day on it to have that needed perk, the mini fridge being the restaurant from which I'll eat my meals all week: a dull continuum of peanut butter and banana sandwiches, cheese sticks, carrots, apples, mixed nuts, hummus, and dried fruit.

Diet is a real consideration for me. Last time I was here I lost eight pounds in a week due to stress, busyness, and fatigue sapping my appetite. So I created a routine. I wake at 6:30 each morning to shower and dress, and then I force down a banana with bad black coffee from the plastic machine in my motel room. All the while, I'm reviewing my client notes for the day and thinking of how best to lead conversations and how better to earn trust and how better to phrase the delicate content of our most painful, intimate, and crucial conversations. An alarm on my cell phone then interrupts me when it's 7:40, and I brush my teeth again, ever cautious about not wanting to blast my clients with coffee breath as we work together in cramped spaces. And at 7:45 on the dot, I'm pulling out of the motel parking lot, clean, fed, and caffeinated. My mind is oriented to my coming tasks, and I head straight to the detention center.

During the drive to the detention center, my mood is stark. I'm somber, focused. It's my period for readying myself emotionally to spend the next ten hours inside a space dominated by pain, anguish, and injustice.

The constant surveillance is wearying too. I know I'll be on video by the time I turn onto the access road to the gravel parking lot for the detention center. And that's when my back will start to tense, and a dull anxiety will start to throb in my ears like a low, steady drumbeat. My throat will go dry, reminding me to sip my water throughout the day, and my mind will be hyperfocused, single-minded: set to work, case after case, priming as many women as possible for successful interviews.

It's a grueling sprint, and too often heartbreaking. These women and children need so much more than a little time with me and a relatively brief interview with an asylum officer deciding their fate.

I carry the strain of it in my body. Over the years I've grown to recognize it. It happens to me everywhere I work with detained people, whether adults or children, whether in prisons or immigrant detention centers, whether in the United States or abroad.

I suppose it's my way of coping, my way of trying to brace myself for that first, harsh slap of entering a place that cages human beings. And then to remain there, working feverishly every minute to serve the detained people until my precious time with them elapses.

It's all the more heartbreaking when remembering that these women and children are destitute and desperate refugees. They should be welcomed and nourished by our national community, not incarcerated as if convicted criminals. That's how they're treated here throughout their detention, where they're stripped of identity, forced into uniforms, pinned in place, intimidated, and muted. Their eyes pulsate with the despair of it all. Their bodies radiate suffering the way the desert here radiates heat.

It's in their broken postures, their jerky movements, their tremulous voices when they dare to speak their truth. I heard it just this morning in the woman pleading with a guard for medicine for her ten-year-old daughter, who's had a headache and diarrhea for three days, adding they'd been twice already to the health clinic but neither time could get seen.

And I heard it in another mother this morning pleading with another guard, this time just outside the door to my team's office in the trailer. I was coming in first thing in the morning, looking to store my briefcase and pick up my first client, when through the flimsy wall I overheard her asking a guard for help for her sick son. Leaving the office I saw the toddler: a boy of two or three, slumped across her lap, his nose crusted green, his breathing wheezy as he napped there. The guard, a tall, irritable man with a shaved head and thick mustache, finally barked at her to take the child to the bathroom to clean his nose. I wondered what the mother's second child, a boy of seven or eight, sitting beside her, taking all of it silently in, thought of the world of adults, of the people here, of the United States, of me.

Every detained person in here is suffering, whether young or old. It ranges from a crusty nose to being haunted by memories of surviving and fleeing genocide.

Each detained person, if trusting you, will courageously share her tragedy with you, will share the scalding details, if available to her, of her story of migration and detention. She also will intimate her suspended dreams for a better future, which she still guards vigilantly. And that's what keeps her going. It's what my team and I are working to support.

Among these brave dreamers is Marta. Her eyes are downcast as she finally resumes speaking. Her legs are crossed at the knee, and her tapping foot on the floor betrays her anxiety as we resume discussing her case. We pore over it in agonizing detail, as we must, acutely aware we have but hours to ready it for the asylum officer.

And words fail to render her sense of urgency, the depth of her pain, and her unrelenting despair in being trapped in this facility, in the immigration system. She is exhausted, having fled Marco, survived bouncing around Mexico alone to escape abuses, and now found herself locked in this strange place. I try to touch her pain as minimally as necessary, which is still excruciating. I'm amazed by her resilience, her stamina, her grit in persevering. And I'm grateful she trusts my team, that she's working with me. It's her best shot at making it through.

In the meantime, she must suffer. It's by design. The detention center is structured in a way that creates despondence in the detained women and their children. It's not only the oppressive weight of feeling criminalized, caged, monitored, recorded, and told even how to clean your own body. It's also the looming threat of deportation: that you could be sent back to the violence, poverty, and misery you were so desperate to escape by migrating in the first place.

Plus, this site is infamous, and the refugees know it. It's where little Mariee Juárez fell gravely ill in 2018, as a nineteen-month-old baby in detention with her young mother, Yasmin.[1] Rumors are that Yasmin repeatedly begged the guards for medical help for Mariee while watching her child wither slowly, painfully, in front of her. Her death was so devastating that it brought Representative Alexandria Ocasio-Cortez to tears a year later, during Yasmin's heartbreaking testimony at a House Oversight subcommittee hearing on family detention. (Allegations against the facility were investigated, but the company was not held responsible for her death.)

It bears mention, too, that this facility is not some dark creation of President Donald Trump. Rather, it was built in 2014, under President Barack Obama, and it is run by a private company, CoreCivic. CoreCivic operates it by way of a federal contract from US Immigration and Customs Enforcement (ICE), under the authority of DHS. In fact, in its first two years alone, the facility collected $261 million in DHS contracts.[2]

Against their detention, my legal team toils away in here via an ever-changing cadre of volunteers. We're mostly lawyers and law students; I'm the rare poet and professor. Another volunteer is a graduate student in psychology. Still another is a retired school teacher and elected leader on her county school board. In total we number eleven people this week, hailing from disparate points across the country. Only eight of us speak Spanish, which is the predominant language of our clients, though I've seen women in here from Brazil, Vietnam, Jordan, Cameroon, Angola, and elsewhere around the globe, not to mention the many women who speak indigenous languages as their primary tongue, like Marta, who speaks Q'anjob'al.

Regardless of language, each woman's voice is ribboned with a dark melody of pain. It's the sound of trauma in human voice, the sound of unyielding, irreparable hurt. And you can discern it in conversation with every detained woman in here. You hear it laced through her speech, the language immaterial. The agony just below the surface, the trauma unyielding.

And secondary trauma is very real too. It's why I go to therapy back home in Virginia. For whom would it *not* be difficult to hear a mother explain how she was tied to a chair in her kitchen and forced to watch her ten-year-old daughter gang-raped on their dinner table?

In that case, the violence was perpetrated because the girl had refused to carry drugs into her elementary school, wanting to be left alone, to play and study. Her father told the drug dealers as much, and then the gang showed up at their front door.

Such stories aren't uncommon. The women tell them plainly, their trauma that deep and encompassing. But for a volunteer, each new story lands like a punch to her gut, leaving her doubled over, gasping for breath. Her heart rattles behind her rib cage, skipping and skittering, having lost its rhythm, before it gradually quiets back down and reasserts a more regular beat. Only then can she recompose herself, reclaim focus, and resume the interview.

But the story remains lodged in her mind, a burning hot metal splinter in her brain. How could it not resurge, whether in the volunteer's dreams or in her daily life, as she moves about her hometown long after having worked in here?

It's difficult to hear a teen explain to you how she watched her father get shot in the face on their porch by masked men one sunny afternoon. Her father, killed right there, sitting beside her, falling slumped across her.

She remembers his blood on her lap, his blood on her shoes, and everything silent, the gunman running off as if in slow motion. And why the murder? Because he'd refused to pay a gang a weekly extortion to keep his bakery open. It was the family business, run from their home, and they were barely making ends meet before the extortion.

And it's difficult to hear a teen mother explain how her toddler son and she were kidnapped, held for three days, how they were beaten, starved, and sexually abused—both of them. And how, when no ransom came, they were blindfolded, loaded into a vehicle, then thrown from it, still moving. She still remembers hearing her boy cry when he landed, and how the sound flooded her with gratitude because hearing his cry meant he'd survived, and she had too.

Those are but three details from three much more complex, agonizing stories of three migrating women's lives now suspended in this detention center.

That is also to say that they represent but three cases of the thousands my team will work this year, not to mention the hundreds of thousands more that will go unheard by advocates like us, the women receiving no legal guidance at all, and therefore more likely to be deported. The injustices in our immigration system are legion. The violence and the cruelty in the world are staggering.

Take Marta's case, for example. She's just now detailing to me how and why she can't return to Mexico. It is precisely why she has a credible fear of returning, which means by law she is entitled to seek asylum here in the United States.

Her cheeks are soaked with her fear, the tears flowing as if unrelated to her narration. They run steadily down her cheek, as if unnoticed by her, while she concentrates on getting out her story as we've discussed, in chronological order, clearly enunciated.

But she's finding it hard to speak. Her throat has tightened, reducing her voice to a whisper. But a whisper is still speech. Each word is filled with a visceral pain, Marta squirming in her plastic chair to endure it. Her autobiography is clear, detailed, compelling, and incontrovertible. I'm optimistic she'll win her case if the official interview goes this way.

Digging deeper still, she closes her eyes, slowly explains how she's nowhere safe in Mexico, how she's everywhere targeted, everywhere abused. Everywhere she's subject to violence for being poor, indigenous, female, and gay, and for being alone. And here in the United States, she could make friends, go to school, learn a trade, get a job, and live in relative safety. Ideally, she'd like to become an elementary school teacher or a nurse, though she'd be happy for any honest work, including manual labor. But those two professions are the two she dreams of, and they're but two of her many, sunny dreams.

Marta also dreams of being less afraid of being gay in public.

She dreams of learning English.

She dreams of learning to ride a bicycle, and maybe even buying one.

She dreams of living in a house with a gate and a locking front door. A house with reliable electricity and with plenty of food, even without a garden, though she'd like one too.

And if she returns to her village, she explains, Marco will kill her. That's a certainty. He's told everyone as much, including her parents. He's boasted, too, of killing Lisbeth. He says he killed her for betraying their marriage vows and for living immorally by sleeping with a woman. And he's hissed to many that Marta is next. She best not show her face. He'll kill her on sight for having "turned" his wife gay, destroying his marriage.

"And despite his confession," she says, shaking her head, looking at the floor, "nothing has been done to him."

We go silent.

Then she adds, "And nothing will be done when he kills me."

She speaks with a burning clarity, with lucid truth. It shakes me to my core. I'll be flabbergasted if she doesn't win her case this afternoon. She most certainly should.

And she's not done talking. She wants to tell me more of the terror of her journey and of her time in US custody.

She explains how she left her village in the dark of night, without a word to anyone, and wandered directionless, penniless, and alone. Day after day, she staggered about, in desperate need of any sort of kindness, finding none.

Instead she met cruelty. She tells how she'd been forced to change course by every act of violence suffered. She'd been beaten, robbed, groped, and chased off like a stray cur. Like this she'd pinballed around her country, finding solace nowhere.

She'd been booted from shelters, encampments, parks, churches, abandoned buildings, and refuges, and whether in villages, towns, or cities, and whether by citizens, police, locals, or fellow migrating people.

Marta found no aid, no sanctuary. Here a priest in his church cursed her sexuality and kicked her out. There a policeman slurred her for her dark skin. Everywhere she was punished for who she is. Everywhere was a temporary place to at best catch her breath before the beatings resumed. Everywhere her head ached, and her heart ached with the bitter noise of homophobic and racist fear like the sound of an angry mob growing nearer and nearer.

So she was tired, worn-out, battered, and afraid. She'd been called every slur for a dark-skinned person. For an Indigenous person. For a gay person. For a woman. And she was at her wits end when one scorching afternoon about a week ago, who knows where, the sky bright blue, when she entered a park in search of a water fountain, skittish as a thirsty bird at a watering hole with lurking predators.

Halfway through the park, still searching, her throat still parched, burning, she bumped into a kind old man in a cowboy hat selling *paletas* from a cart.

He took pity on Marta, handed her an ice-cold bottle of water. He told her, too, that a US state called Texas was but three kilometers from where they stood, and that Texas might have more water and even food and shelter for a person like her. Thanking him, she wandered off in that general direction. But she found no state, only a wide and fast river, stopping her in place under the punishing sun.

Not knowing what else to do, she jumped in, forgetting she didn't know how to swim. She was that tired, that desperate, that broken and confused. And that unaware of the sharp undertow, and the swift current rushing downriver.

She began to struggle, swallowing water in big gulps that drowned her cries for help. Slipping under, she'd pop up, only to be pulled under again, tumbling through darkness. Then the light again, the bright, blue sky, the sun a glaring, golden eye.

She was being yanked, tugged sideways. She was being fished out of the river by a pair of men. They were dressed in green military uniforms. She remembers being terrified of them.

They were US Border Patrol agents, though she didn't know it. All she knew was there were two of them. She knew they were tall and broad-shouldered. She knew both had mustaches and dark sunglasses, and that both were shouting at her incomprehensibly, like two dogs barking with frothing lips.

She tried to listen, tried to understand, but she was in shock, from the near drowning. And they spoke a disordered kind of Spanish, pocked with odd words and a strange accent. She could tell it wasn't their first language. Nor was it hers.

On shore in a sopping heap at their feet, she coughed and sucked air while thanking them profusely in *Q'anjob'al* for saving her, not realizing that she was speaking in her native tongue, nor why they were looking at her with baffled faces.

And although they'd just helped her, she still feared them. She feared their green uniforms. She feared the black radios on their shoulders, the pistols on their hips. It all reminded her of the military men who'd sporadically raided her village throughout her childhood, whether agents of the Mexican state or its sworn enemies, seeking supplies, food, women. Regardless, the result was always the same: a bloody rampage, brazen theft, and a shattered village.

So she tried to stay alert with these two men in green despite her fatigue, the adrenaline surge waning.

She tried to think of ways to protect herself and flee, despite her zip-tied wrists.

She wondered if she was about to be raped and killed, then dumped in this desert. Were these her final hours?

She shuddered with fear as the back of one man's hand grazed her chin as he tipped a canteen of warm water to her lips.

After she drank, they pushed her into the backseat of a white and green truck with sirens on its roof. Between the air conditioning and her wet clothes, she began to shiver with cold. She grew angry with herself, self-reproachful, for letting them see her unable to control her body, something they'd surely note as a sign of weakness, exploit later.

On they sped down the dirt road in a sun-scorched expanse of vacant desert. Despondent, jittery with fatigue, she looked out the window in silence. A large, black bird appeared, and she watched it land on a ragged sage bush. She took it as an omen of violence to come. She dropped her head between her knees and thought of Lisbeth.

She wished Lisbeth were there, holding her hand, smiling softly into her eyes. She imagined being shoulder to shoulder with her in the backseat, their warm bodies bobbing along with the truck as it bumped and skidded down the dirt road.

Given all she'd suffered, all she'd seen, Marta needed the fantasy. Concurrently, she began preparing herself for a vicious end, thinking it frightening but also a kind of release.

Then just as suddenly as she'd been fished from the river, the truck slid to a stop in a cloud of dust. The driver killed the engine. Marta heard a jangle of keys, and one of the men in green was abruptly pulling her from the vehicle.

He grunted something she didn't understand and began pushing her towards a small, squat building. It was some kind of military outpost or guerrilla base, Marta thought. It was the very place where she'd be murdered.

Once inside, though, she felt differently. It was air-conditioned, bureaucratic, and orderly. Its large central room was filled with soft yellow lighting, under which more men in green uniforms worked, alone at computers or in clusters, conversing quietly.

An unsmiling secretary met Marta and her guards just inside the front door. She was sitting at a computer, too, ready and waiting. She spat a few, rapid-fire questions in good Spanish at Marta—name, nationality, birthdate, are you traveling alone—and then passed her on to a new man in a green uniform at a desk about ten feet behind hers.

He was an older man with pink skin, blue eyes, and a gray mustache like a silkworm moth hovering over his lips. He indicated that Marta should sit, which she did, and then he interviewed her much like the secretary. He asked for her name, nationality, birthdate, and if she was traveling alone or with a group. Making her blush deeply with confusion, he asked also about her health, and if she had a fear of returning to Mexico.

His Spanish was fitful, coming in bursts of slurred, inscrutable phrases. She understood little of what he said, and she spoke mostly by nodding, even if it were nonsensical. And she kept blushing with confusion and turning her eyes away from him wherever he'd look up at her from his paperwork. Finally, he rose from his desk and led her by the elbow into a windowless holding cell, already packed with other migrating people.

There he released her from her zip ties; she rubbed her wrists and furtively surveyed the room. A dozen tired faces stared back at her, their eyes scared. No one said a word.

Hours later (or was it the next morning?), Marta woke on the floor, disoriented by sleep, struggling to grasp where she was.

As her mind came clear, she noticed that the number of people around her had doubled, maybe tripled. Moments later, a man in green banged on the cell door with a baton, then herded them single file onto a bus waiting out front of the building.

It took them to a *hielera,* or ice-cold holding facility. Marta spent two or three freezing nights there on a bare concrete floor. She was with about twenty other women and their children inside a big cage with a locked door. Each of them had been given a foil blanket, their only possession. There was a single toilet for them to share. The men had been separated out and imprisoned elsewhere. The teen boys too.

If the women spoke at all in here, they mostly whispered nervously after any news of the whereabouts of their husbands and sons. No one knew anything. With a twinge of guilt, Marta felt a rush of gratitude that she'd migrated alone. At least she was spared the slow-burning agony of these wives and mothers, missing their loved ones, wondering where and how they were, and if they'd been deported.

In the *hielera*, Marta soon lost track of time. She knew its passage only by the strange meals that punctuated her shivering under her foil blanket throughout the days. Those meals featured stale bread with what she described as gray discs of floppy, thin meat. She'd never seen anything like it, but she ate each sandwich appreciatively: grateful for the distraction, the nutrition, and the soft bumper against her clattering teeth.

At times, to savor the meal further, she'd imagine sharing her sandwich with Lisbeth. She'd imagine them taking alternating bites. She could even hear Lisbeth chew. And she took pleasure in imagining how they'd nap after the meal, side by side under their foil blankets, cozying their bodies together and regaining strength.

Before daybreak and without explanation, Marta was jerked from the cell half-asleep. Groggy and confused, she marched along in a line with several other women and children. They were boarded onto a new bus, this time arriving at what looked like a military camp in a desert, everything silvery white. It was Dilley. She knew neither her location nor the date. All she knew was that she was scared, tired, and too weak to try to resist.

She drifted through her check-in interviews here like a ghost, barely listening and saying very little. Soon an officer in a maroon uniform was leading her to a cot, which she understood to be hers. Throwing herself down on it, she fell deeply asleep atop its scratchy blanket. It was bliss to be left alone. She remembered dreaming of being free in the United States, joyfully safe, living with Lisbeth.

When she woke, a golden light filtered through the nearby window, glowed in the room. A young mother, María Luisa, struck up a conversation from the next cot over. She explained to Marta the date, where they were, the daily schedule, and the personality of each guard and how best to approach them. And it was from María Luisa that Marta learned, too, of the availability of free legal aid from US lawyers.

"They have an air-conditioned trailer near the front of the detention center," she said. "And we're always welcome there."

The next morning Marta wandered into our trailer, and here we sit, in the greasy plastic chairs in this stuffy interview room.

She finishes telling me about María Luisa, and I ask her if she has any more questions for me. She nods no, says she understands she must tell her story completely, truthfully, and slowly, and then crosses her fingers.

I reiterate that I think her case is strong. I tell her, too, that we never know how it will go; all she can do is try. And that she's well prepared, that she'll do her part well, but to be ready, too, for the worst-case scenario. Should she get a bad result, then she'll be scheduled for deportation, likely in a day or two. No matter what, though, I told her to please come back to see me after the interview, if she'd like. I explain that it often helps our clients, who too frequently leave the interview confused and worried, not understanding the outcome, asking us if they've lost or won, and will they be deported?

Marta again nods her understanding. I sense she's ready to leave. She's surely drained. We've been in this stuffy interview room for two hours now. I rise to signal the end, not wanting her to feel awkward about asking if we can conclude.

Standing there face to face, I remind her that, most importantly, she should remember to breathe, no matter what's happening. Seeing the fear in her eyes, I quickly add that it's normal to feel nervous, lonely, and worried, and that she's an amazingly strong and resilient person.

As we bid farewell, I add that my team is always here to help, Monday through Thursday, 8:30–5:30. And I suggest that she use the next few hours to try to eat something, rest on her cot, and arrive punctually for her interview, having gone to the bathroom prior to it.

Before we separate, I say again that her case is compelling. That she's ready. That she's a strong, amazing person who can do this, and I'm honored to have met her and hope she'll keep fighting for her dreams.

At that, her mouth twists into a half-smile. I cross my arms and pat both my shoulders. It's the signal I'd told her about at the beginning of our interview, which meant that I was hugging her without touching.

She smiles at me, and I at her. She thanks me in Spanish and *Q'anjob'al* and walks out the door.

I linger over my yellow notepad, jotting down a few final thoughts before collecting my things from the desk, completely unaware that I'll never again see Marta.

The next afternoon, anxious for news, I'll learn she lost her case, was scheduled for deportation. And that will be it. I'll hurry to our break room, turn my face to a wall, and hide my tears.

Five minutes later, recomposed, I'll be back in the stuffy interview room, but with a new client, a young Guatemalan mother with a sick toddler, no more than age two. Thoughts of Yazmin and Mariee Juárez will leap to mind. Thoughts of Marta and Lisbeth will ghost through too. But I'll force myself to focus on the present, on this teary mother, just now reaching for a tissue, her story already spilling out: how her ex, a high-ranking gang member, was trying to steal her baby from her.

He wanted sole custody, so that he could raise the child with his new girlfriend, inside their compound. To prove he was deadly serious, he'd shot up the front of her house one night. He then beat her brother in the street to make himself even more clear: the baby was his, hand him over. And when that didn't work, he threatened her boss at the tortilla shop to fire her, so she'd go hungry. Finally, he'd barged into her home late one night and put a gun to her head, shouting he was taking the child. Thankfully, he was so high on drugs that he soon passed out cold on her couch, his gun slipping to the floor.

She crept past him there, past the gun, with her son in her arms. The two of them fled Guatemala that very night, heading north, hoping to outrun the gang and its transcontinental network, which by the next day was already circulating her photo by text among all the *clicas* from Guatemala to the United States, and with orders to kidnap her and the child on site and send the boy back to Guatemala City.

Along the way, she'd lost the route. She was robbed at gunpoint—*they even took my baby's shoes*—and ended up here, in detention with her toddler, the two of them locked up like criminals, like the gang members they were fleeing, and could I please help them?

CHAPTER 5

~~~~

The Deepest Darkness

You must write, and read, as if your life depended on it.

— ADRIENNE RICH

Daniel was on his knees last night, trembling, in the dark beside his bed. Plagued by insomnia, he couldn't stop thinking about his mother.

Maybe it was because his sixteenth birthday was coming up, a sad occasion in a juvenile immigration detention center, something Daniel had never before experienced. So he was thinking of his mother.

He had been scouring his mind for any happy memory of their life together, no matter how hazy or distant. But he'd had no luck. Even before her death, his childhood had been a steady stream of misery and deprivation. His neighborhood in San Salvador was rough, as had been his mother with him, so he'd slogged through days filled with poverty, neglect, violence, and death. And it was why in a poetry workshop a few weeks back, he'd fallen in love with the line "I was born on a day that God was sick."

It had come in a poem by César Vallejo that the group was discussing, and it hit Daniel like a lightning strike, leaving him suddenly illuminated in his seat, ablaze. He burst out in spontaneous praise for the poetry of it, saying how the line spoke for him, as if he'd written it. He said it was exactly how he felt. He said, yes, he, too, was born on a day God was sick.

All around him, his peers nodded. Several added "*Eso*" and "'*tá bueno*." And it was true. Daniel had always felt like this, though he had never before known how to articulate it. Now, with Vallejo's words, he now knew how to name the sucking emptiness that for so long had haunted him. He felt abandoned by God, just as he felt abandoned by his mother.

A devout Christian, she had thrown him out of the house at age fourteen for running the streets with a gang. It was a brutal blow. They would never again live together, though neither of them could have known it in that explosive moment of parting.

She had simply had enough of his behavior. She harbored no patience for sinning. And for her, gang life was the epitome of sin.

That is why she had warned him sternly throughout his elementary-school years to avoid the gangs as the devil. She had taken him to church with her and prayed for his salvation. She demanded he pray for it, too: on his knees beside the bed every morning upon waking up and every night before going to sleep.

So when he came home with a fresh, green gang tattoo on his hand, it was the last straw. She lost it. She saw it as a literal mark of the devil, a permanent pledge to sin, and she kicked him out of the house. In their final exchange, she had hissed that she wouldn't have "street trash" under her roof.

Still he loved her; she was his mother. But he loved the gang too. And his love for the gang only grew after her funeral. The gang helped him to survive, day after day, on the streets of a city that had been labeled the murder capital of the world. And the gang felt like an extended family, something he had never known, having had only his mother in this world. She had not always been kind to him.

Plus, he felt he *belonged* on the street. Where else could he fit in? He felt unfit for school, having dropped out in fifth grade, and he felt unfit for work, having neither job skills nor experience.

At least that is what he thought until his mom died, about a year and a half after kicking him out. Despite all their problems, despite all his resentments, her death shook him to his core. He decided then and there to change his life. He wanted to get off the streets, go back to school. He wanted to get a job, learn a trade, live in safety and peace.

But to do so, he knew that he would need to leave the gang, which was almost impossible. His only options were to find God or flee. He could either feign a religious rebirth or leave El Salvador completely. To do the former, he would need to begin to do good works in the community to prove his faith in public and regularly to the gang, which *might* accept his faith as justification for his leaving. Alternatively, he'd have to emigrate to escape the gang's reach. A reach that extended across the entirety of the country via an intricate network of interwoven *clicas*, all of which would receive his photo by text message and be greenlit to kill him for abandoning the gang without permission.

He chose the latter option and fled, at first on foot, then hopping a bus, a truck, and finally a train. Two weeks later, he was wandering, lost, in a scorching desert, until crossing paths with US Border Patrol agents and ending up in here, locked up, lonely, and desperate, with a birthday drawing near.

That was what he was thinking about last night. It was why he could not sleep. It was what had driven him to his knees, where battling unrelenting ghosts, he had trembled for hours in unrelenting grief. It is also why this morning in workshop, exhausted, his eyes red and bleary, he wrote the following poem.

No quiero hacer nada
Quisiera ver a mi mamá,
Pero no era buena conmigo.
Nunca me dijo te quiero,
Que yo era de la calle.
Siempre quisiera que me quiera.
Quiero que me digas soy tuyo, hijo,
Que tú me amas,
Pero no porque está muerta.
Pero yo me siento nada,
No me importa la vida de ella...

Siempre en mi cuarto me pongo a llorar.
El ver mucha lluvia es como lloro en mi cuarto.
Siempre estoy en la noche pidiéndole a Dios
Que me diera una madre que sí me quiera.

"¡Padre nuestro Jesús Nazareno!
Al considerar vuestra bondad
Y vuestro amor para mí,
Un grito de gratitud sale de mis labios,
Diciéndolos
¡Jesus mio, os amo!
Por nuestro amor bajasteis a la tierra
Y sufristeis dolores acerbisimos,
Muriendo clavado en una cruz,
Por nuestro amor os disteis como manjar
En el sacramento de nuestros altares,
Por nuestro amor
Os manifestáis en esa imagen bendita,

coronado de espinas,
con los ojos lánguidos y el rostro dolorido,
símbolo de vuestro sufrimiento.
¡Gracias, Señor!
Y para corresponder a tantos favores
Os pido la gracia
De cumplir siempre vuestra ley santa
Y de morir en vuestro amor
Amen."

Porque lo pido Dios,
Pa'que me de una madre.

I don't want to do anything . . .
I'd have liked to see my mom,
But she wasn't good to me.
She never told me I love you,
she called me a street kid.
I'd always wanted her to love me,
I want you to tell me I'm yours, son,
That you love me.
But it won't happen because she's dead.
And I don't feel anything,
Her life doesn't matter to me. . .

In my cell I always cry.
My crying in my cell is like heavy rain.
At night I always ask God
To give me a mother that loves me.

"Our Father, Jesus of Nazareth!
Considering your goodness
And your love for me,

A cry of gratitude escapes my lips,
Telling you,
Dear Jesus, I love you!
For our love, you descended to Earth
And you suffered bitter pain,
Dying nailed to a cross,
For our love, you gave us the sacrament
Of our alters to feast on,
For our love,
You appeared in that blessed image,
Crowned with thorns,
With sad eyes and a sorrowing face,
The symbol of your suffering.
Thank you, God!
And to repay so many favors
I beg you the grace
To always uphold your holy law
And die in your love.
Amen."

I ask this of you, God,
So that you'll give me a mother.

The poem reveals a child in existential despair. He is deep in desperate prayer, begging God for a mother. It is among the most primal human urges: that of a child in distress to reach for his mother. And it is a heartbreaking gesture in the context of this poem.

First and foremost, it is heartbreaking here because the poet is reaching impossibly for a mother who is dead. He is yearning for her to comfort him, wishing for her to soothe him by telling him, "I love you" and saying, "I'm yours, son."

More heartbreakingly still, even were she alive, that comfort would not come. In life "she wasn't good to [him]." Yet he still wants her love, and that, too, is heartbreaking.

Additionally, he is making this prayer for a mother. Making a prayer from an isolation cell deep within a maximum-security juvenile immigration detention center in a remote rural valley. He is unreachable in this new country, even had his Salvadoran mother traveled to be near him here.

Thus, for mortal, relational, legal, geographical, and logistical reasons, he is utterly isolated from any adult who might wish to lovingly take him to their breast as son and shower him with unconditional love. Moreover, he is a child yearning for an unconditional love that he has never known. And that is heartbreaking too. He is praying for the chance to sample for the first time what is a fundamental given for most children throughout their childhood.

Against that lack of unconditional love, to defy its absence from his life, he has tried to find it on his own: first by joining the gang, and then by migrating to the United States. Neither attempt has succeeded—at least not to date.

Most nights he is unable to sleep in here. He weeps in the dark of his cell. He kneels for hours, begging his God for mercy. But there is little mercy in this place.

That is also to say that his situation is by no means unique in this detention center, nor in any other facility incarcerating undocumented, unaccompanied youth. As evident in our every workshop, and in reports on children in immigration detention across the nation, suffering is as pervasive as mercy is absent.

Take for example the poem below as further proof. It is by Rafael, yet another child in existential crisis in this detention center, and his suffering, too, is severe.

This time it just so happens that the child-poet is Mexican. Rafael is also younger than Daniel, but much more muscular.

This has perhaps led to him being ever more unfairly profiled as dangerous, and he is quick to share a long list of mistreatment in recent years, whether by the Mexican police or the US immigration system.

Rafael's existential struggle is also more self-destructive and more public than Daniel's. His anger often simmers just behind his eyes like a flickering wildfire. I can see the hurt that fuels this rage, though he tries to hide that deeper truth by wearing a hard outer disposition on the cellblock. It makes him difficult to reach for most people, hurting his ability to find friendship and support from his peers, although that is precisely what he so desperately needs. And with the guards, he can be downright surly and defiant. A few times this has led them to punish him by refusing to let him out of his cell for our workshop.

But with me, one-on-one, he's gentle, open, both in conversation and writing. He and I connect because of and through poetry. It sparks for us good and ranging conversations, as a loving uncle might have with his nephew.

Consequently, across our many months together, Rafael has confided in me that he wants to go to school. That he wants to learn English. That he wants to become a mechanic or maybe a chef. That he wants to get married one day (though "not too soon!" he laughs). That he wants to have children. And I know he loves soccer and rap music and tacos, especially *de carne asada*. I also know that like Daniel, Rafael is deeply wounded, and he suffers from a profound absence of love in his life, as this poem of his makes clear in brutal detail.

Sin título
Antes yo pensaba que podría encontrar
una persona que realmente me quiera.
¿Por qué decía yo que lo encontraría

si mi madre no me quiera?
No puedo encontrar a alguien que
me quiera.
Mi papá lo mataron. No tenía
nadie. No tenía casa. No tenía
nada. Vivía en la calle.
Siento un vacío en mí porque
no tengo nadie. Tengo una tía
pero no es igual. Quiero mi
papá. Quiero mi mamá.
A mí no me importa la vida.
Me importa mi familia. Iba a la
cárcel dos veces. Pero no me
importa. Cuando salgo de aquí,
quiero vivir en los EEUU con
mi tía.
Cuando estoy en mi cuarto
pienso en estas cosas. I cut myself.
Peleo con los chicos y me ponen
en mi cuarto.
Me entran ganas de llorar pero no
puedo.

Untitled
I used to believe that I'd be able to find
someone who'd really love me.
Why did I say I'd find someone
when my own mother didn't love me?
I can't find anyone
who loves me.
They killed my father. I didn't have
anyone. I didn't have a house. I didn't have
anything. I lived in the street.

I feel an emptiness in me because
I don't have anyone. I have one aunt
but it's not the same. I want my
dad. I want my mom.
My life doesn't matter to me.
My family matters to me. I went
to jail twice. But I don't
care. When I get out of here,
I want to live in the United States with
my aunt.
When I'm in my cell
I think of these things. I cut myself.
I fight with the other kids, so they throw me
back in my cell.
I want to cry but I
can't.

Here is a child who wants to run from detention in order to find love and freedom, but he can't. His frustration is enormous. His anguish is nearly unbearable.

To vent the pressure from those tormenting feelings, he injures himself in his cell. And when forced from that cell, he is prone to start fights in order to ensure his swift return to it, wherein he will resume cutting himself. It's an ouroboros of suffering. And it is all too familiar in places like this.

This is the damage we knowingly and repeatedly impose on child refugees by incarcerating them. Much the same is true of adults in ICE detention. Sadly, too, these are foreseeable outcomes from forcing already desperate and traumatized people to live under these conditions. And it need not be this way. We can structure life differently for migrating people, including these child refugees. We can change our immigration policies and practices to help, not harm them. And maybe that would help to lift Daniel from his bruised knees and to sleep. Maybe it would help to quell the wildfire raging in Rafael's heart, and in the hearts of so many children suffering similarly within the system.

Quite understandably, the pressure on these children is immense. Some might even say it's unreasonable, sadistic, and cruel. The children grow weary and sick from the weight of it. Their desperation grows exponentially by the day. Some even attempt suicide, as the following poet discusses through the supportive space of workshop.

This time the poet, Maynor, is a Honduran child. He is surprisingly gregarious and talkative in workshop each week for someone so forlorn and hurting. He is a skinny boy, almost wiry, and he often perches folded into himself on his stool like an eagle instead of sitting on it (most of the children do). Like this he listens attentively to his peers, all the while bristling with an unsettled energy, and he watches everything with his almond-shaped eyes, constantly surveying the room and scanning the faces of the guards and his peers, rarely missing a thing.

He also is a fabulous lyricist. He often recites his original rap songs from memory, much to the delight of the group. But nothing abates the sucking emptiness he feels. It engulfs his days and haunts his nights, suffocating him minute by minute until he acts against himself.

From deep within that choking pain, he found it within himself one morning in a workshop on the theme of survival to summon the following poem.

Sin título

*Me he intentado suicidar 6 veces pero ninguna con
éxito, pero sé que tarde o noche tendrá que llegar el
momento que de un trompezón se me vaya la vida*

*por eso no anhelo ser un poeta o un científico o un
pastor o un presidente o ser alguien prestigiado porque
de qué me sirve saber tanto si con un golpe en la
cabeza olvidaría todo ni tan siquiera me acordaría
de mi nombre.*

Untitled

I tried to kill myself 6 times without succeeding, but
I know that day or night the moment will have to
come when from a fall I'll lose my life and that's why
I don't long to become a poet or scientist or pastor
or president or to be someone prestigious because
what's the point of knowing so much if with a blow
to the head I'd forget everything unable even to
remember my name.

Like so many other children in this place, this poet is grap-
pling with depression. In his case, he is also suicidal. He has
little hope, and he wants only an end to his suffering, even if
by his own hand.

Whatever its details, he expects his death to be violent. It
might come from his seventh suicide attempt. It might come
from someone jumping him and delivering a fatal blow to the
head. Such is his existential despair and his sense of his own
fragility. Imagine the daily anxiety of life for him in here.
Imagine suffering that ever-present anxiety alone.

Worse, however extreme his suffering, it is entirely unsur-
prising. It is the predictable consequence of the conditions of
captivity that he and other children feel in this relentlessly
oppressive place.

The immigration system wants these children to be unable
to see a healthy future, and it wants them to suffer in cold,

stark cells, alone. That is the point of the US immigration paradigm of Prevention Through Deterrence. It is a system predicated on trying to frighten off future migrating people from taking a chance on entering US territories. Because if an undocumented person is lucky enough to dodge death in the desert while migrating, then they will suffer harsh detention in the US carceral system. The ordeal will be brutal, costly, and scarring, and it will most often result anyway in the forced return of the migrating person to their country of origin.

Still, as I'd point out repeatedly to the children, and as I point out here to all readers, there is hope. After all, the refugees recorded their experiences in poetry. Each child, however desperate, *created* something in workshop. It happened to be a poem, because that is the art form that I shared with them. And each of the resulting poems now stands as a materialization of their presence. Each poem affirms its author's existence, recording his experiences and ideas. And that material object can be shared with others, like music. It can be picked up and read, loosing a song, across time and place.

That experience of writing, sharing, and reading poetry thereby ruptures the enforced isolation of the children. Each poem invites its audience to extend and/or initiate new ruptures to that dreaded space of oppression.

More intimately, through a poem, and through the exchange of many subsequent poems, the children in a cellblock can connect with one another. They can trace one another's hearts and cherish their expanded understandings of what it is to exist in here, after so much suffering, and it can help them to imagine alternative futures, perhaps ones with alternatives to self-harm or suicide. And they can carry one another forward, even dissociated as they are, by being forced to live in isolation cells.

In other words, by making a poem, a child marks their presence in the world, which was and is something these children fear under their current conditions of erasure as inmates. And then the child can offer that assertion of existing, of being, to other children in here as a point of mutually nourishing interpersonal connection, and it can at times be sustaining, even if only briefly.

Moreover, that act of making, however ephemeral, involves deep introspection, creativity, courage, and generosity of spirit. In this sense, then, the act of poetry writing can be understood as the opposite of suicide. Poetry is an act against dying. It is an assertion of life in the face of suicidal impulses and suicidal conditions. And it is also a conduit of community, encouraging a network of fellowship to support each child amidst their shared besiegement of spirit.

Thus, through poetry, however melancholic and hopeless in theme at times, these children can assert that they *are*, and they can exchange such affirmations with every member of the workshop in our every meeting.

Quite literally, too, while engaged in workshop, the children are specifically not in their cells, cutting themselves, or attempting suicide. And that, too, is a significant benefit of our activity together.

More deeply, it is another sign that our workshops can function simultaneously on both existential and physical planes, affecting both the mind and body, and thereby influencing lived experience, however minutely or ephemerally.

The workshop generates hope by being something that the children can look forward to. They look forward to our time together, and that small hope can help them through their days too. They tell me as much in workshop, often effusing over moments of enjoyment in the experience. They'll share how proud they are of their new piece of writing or how much they enjoyed reading their partner's poem that day or how much they enjoyed hearing a certain poem read aloud or how much they simply enjoy the candy that I pass out during each visit. And all of that contributes to their pleasure in our time together, however abbreviated and inadequate to the overall health and well-being of a child.

These children first and foremost need robust and consistent healthcare from trained and accredited healthcare professionals. It should be foundational to the infrastructure of their time in the care of the state. Some children in workshop even ask explicitly for it, writing of their depression, discussing self-harm, and asking about possibilities for therapy, psychiatry, and psychopharmacology from well-resourced bilingual-Spanish healthcare professionals, whom they lament as lacking.

This is to say, too, that the agony of detention is crushing and relentless. It also is unnecessary. Still the children suffer acutely every day, and no poem could protect them from that or end it. But there are interventions that could be introduced to improve the well-being of child refugees in the care of the state. They would change the lived conditions of the children, and those changes would also shift the national character of the state to one of benevolence, hospitality, and grace.

Most definitely, no poetry workshop could undo the structural violence of the US immigration system. No poem could transform life for a child trapped in the viciousness of a US carceral system that props up US immigration policy with a honeycomb of isolation cells filled with children.

But that policy could be changed, had we the collective desire, will, and vision. And the children's poetry helps us to see the need, just as it helps the children to subsist. Poetry provides them with sporadic flashes of kindness and hope. It protects the dreams in their besieged hearts. It offers them bridges to other children, other lives, and those moments of interpersonal connection are nourishing.

Still, overwhelmingly, the children continue to suffer daily. Yet through and against their agony, these children persist. And within their daily struggle to endure, they very much want to gather, for workshop, to write and share poems. Our workshops buzz with creative energy, and the fruits of the children's heartfelt labor are as impactful and healthy for any audience as for the poet.

This is a testament to the children's character, as well as their potential to help others to live better. Their compassion and diligence in workshop are signs of their resilience, ingenuity, and courage. All of which seem relatively squandered in detention when compared to the lives they might lead in freedom in the United States, much to our collective betterment.

In other words, migrating people and refugees need and deserve far more extensive support than the odd volunteer poetry workshop in one of the nation's hundreds of immigrant detention centers. The current system punishes children such that they are even driven to self-harm and suicidality. Meanwhile, in our workshops, those very children exemplify the ability of diverse migrating people to come together in the United States intimately and supportively, even inside a maximum-security detention center.

Imagine if they weren't incarcerated but instead moving through an immigration system privileging alternatives to detention. How would the small and fleeting successes glimpsed through our weekly poetry workshops, but by no means exclusive to them, be amplified by a broader, systemic commitment to nurturing the humanity of migrating people? Encouraged by the successes of the children in workshop, how could we develop a renovated immigration system focusing on compassion, well-being, encouragement, and community?

What a boon it would be for the nation, including for currently incarcerated children. Such a reorientation to immigration would *grow* the light of the nation by adding the light in these children to it. But to date, we as a nation have seemed unwilling to think fairly about any potential large-scale reconfiguration of our immigration system.

I understand: it is a massive undertaking. The question of transnational migration is complicated. It involves geopolitics, climate change, ethics, complex economics, and legal theory. So we dodge or skim it. We deviate into partial and abbreviated debates about peripheral talking points, which are much easier and quicker to articulate and deal with in our already quite complicated busy lives.

I must immediately add, too, that this is not a partisan complaint. It is by no means an appeal to the relatively superficial designations of party politics in the United States. As aforementioned, this problem is too complex for those narrow, limited skirmishes. It is a far deeper problem than that. It is an international humanitarian crisis.

As such, it cannot and should not be alleged to be the fault of any party or subgroup of the US political infrastructure. Nor is it fair or helpful to consider it a consequence of any particular US president. Rather it is our collective failure, as human beings, and we can redress it, if we so choose.

CHAPTER 6

Digital Activism: The Yin

They spoke to each other in a language as tender as tears.

— DELMIRA AGUSTINI

A nother day, another immigration project. This time the work is virtual. The refugees are already in the United States, but they're incarcerated in immigration detention centers all over the country.

My role is to serve as their Spanish-language interpreter while they work with pro bono immigration attorneys, who don't speak Spanish. And much as the refugees are scattered across the archipelago of the more than 270 facilities spanning the nation, so, too, are the attorneys spread far and wide, in offices anywhere from Hawaii to Washington, D.C.

I myself am in Virginia. Hence our work occurs mostly by telephone. It's typically phone calls that last twenty-five to sixty minutes, and the calls are often preceded and followed by flourishes of emails, texts, and other virtual forms of communication. The mix is necessary to our triangular collaboration across such vast distances on our subtle, delicate, and consequential work, which is as time-sensitive as it is life-changing.

Such is the case this afternoon. I've been recruited for a last-minute phone call. A new client in ICE detention has desperately contacted us to request an urgent meeting. He said it must be today or he'll be deported.

So our program director scrambled to accommodate him, hitting the LISTSERV and phonebank hard. Her work is a near invisible, crucial struggle each day as she hustles her way through call after call to overworked attorneys and paralegals, and the odd bilingual professor like me.

The result is that she's paired me with one of the newest attorneys. He doesn't speak Spanish, and the client is Cuban and speaks no English.

Other than that, all I know is that the attorney is named Ahmed and our client is Esteban, and he's being held in the Otero County Processing Center in Chaparral, New Mexico.

"Stand by to be connected," I hear over the phone, which I have pinned to my ear with one shoulder.

I'm using both of my hands to try to hurry my sons into our kitchen from the garage after picking them up at school.

I'm carrying their backpacks, holding the phone with my shoulder, and begging my boys in whispers to be as quiet as possible. It's the best I can do, having had little time to prepare my schedule for this meeting, and with my wife at work at the hospital until very late this evening.

When I first agreed to this call, I'd really hoped to have at least a minute or two to transition from school pick-up to this phone call. But it wasn't to be. The school pick-up line had been sluggish, and there'd been traffic all the way home.

So here I am, on an urgent phone call with a new client in detention who has a new attorney to boot. This all while also shepherding my sons into the house to get them settled enough for me to work.

On top of this, all around my sons' and my legs, our two small dogs are yapping and weaving. They're wild with joy, bouncing and spinning at our return after a day away.

Amidst all this bustle, my younger son, Joaquín, is also asking me for something to eat.

Before I can answer him, Ahmed breaks in.

"Seth, are you there?" he asks. "Can you hear me?"

I must've worried him when I muted my phone a minute ago while parking my car in the garage. I'd done it precisely because I'd anticipated this calamitously noisy family reunion in the kitchen, which I'd hoped to keep off the phone, squealing dogs and all.

With no choice now, I have to risk unmuting. I try to hush my boys and dogs, then reply with feigned poise and calm, "Yes, I'm here, Ahmed. Good to meet you."

"It's good to meet you too," he says warmly, his voice kind and sincere.

And it's amazing: every last one of the pro bono attorneys with whom I've worked has been like this, exuding a benevolent energy, whatever their personality. Whether serious or wacky, introverted or gregarious, they've all been uncommonly gracious people, even when exhausted and dispirited by the work, which can be excruciating.

Selfishly, that's also a side perk of this type of volunteer work that I really treasure. I've met scores of inspiring, determined attorneys from across the United States and Mexico, and they give me hope for a more just future, when systems of power will respect the dignity of all human beings. At least that's what they're fighting for.

And Ahmed counts among them. His voice is calm and soothing. He speaks in a smooth baritone with a charismatic lilt, which I'll come to learn is a signature of his having grown up in Sarajevo, Bosnia and Herzegovina, where he first became an attorney. He now practices US immigration law just outside Washington, D.C.

As we wait for Esteban to be patched in, Ahmed continues casually, politely.

"Thank you for helping on such short notice," he says, adding with a chuckle, "my Spanish is nonexistent."

"No problem," I say. "Glad to help."

And I wish I could elaborate. I wish I could tell him how deeply I admire and appreciate his volunteering for this project, for this case. And I wish I could tell him how inspired I am by all of the immigration attorneys like him across the United States and in Mexico fighting for immigration justice and reform. But we're live on the phone with the Otero County Processing Center, meaning their staff is listening to us, if not outright recording us. So I play it safe and keep my comments focused, brief, and tonally subdued.

In general, that's my modus operandi as an interpreter. I only speak when interpreting or when directly asked a question. So I fall silent now and hope for a chance to talk with Ahmed in the future, without Otero listening in.

"¿Hola?" a voice cuts in.

It sounds distant and thin. It's also trapped in a bramble of noisy static, making it all the more difficult to hear.

"Hello?" Ahmed asks, but there's no answer, or at least none we can discern.

Everything is static.

I close my eyes to try to hear better, as if that will help, when what I really need is a clean connection, not to mention a dog kennel and a babysitter.

Pushing a handful of string cheeses silently into Joaquín's hand with a smile, I point his brother and him towards their iPads®. With a flurry of hand signals and mouthed words, I suggest that they play games in Spanish until I'm finished.

They're delighted: the rare treat of videogames on a weekday!

Off they happily trot towards the couch to snack and play, with the dogs following, tails wagging, confident in their chances to steal cheese from distracted children.

"Hello?" Ahmed says again through the crackle.

Still nothing. Only static.

"Esteban," he asks again, "can you hear us?"

"*Sí, sí,*" the tinny voice confirms.

And just like that, a new case begins.

It will be filled with heartbreak, joy, frustration, hope, anger, and relief. That's the typical admixture of feelings experienced in these cases as they twist and turn their way through our tumultuous legal system. What varies with each case is the order and intensity of those aforementioned feelings. They combine differently in each client, and consequently in each attorney and me.

At the moment, the predominant sentiment is one of cautious hope. We are new to one another in a dodgy system rife with pain. Thus, we're in an especially delicate and critical juncture: our success as a team will depend upon our ability to trust one another.

For Esteban this is more crucial than he can know. Being newly arrived and detained here, he has no idea that, empirically, studies show incarcerated refugees with attorneys to be as much as ten times more likely to win their cases than those without representation.[1]

So he's off to a good start in having an attorney, but for the partnership to work, trust must be built. It seems auspicious to me, then, that our conversation this afternoon has begun in a kind of bonding, with the client and attorney commiserating over how difficult it is to hear each other.

Ever gracious, Ahmed even apologizes for the static, though it has nothing to do with him.

For his part, Esteban volunteers that some of the background noise is likely due to him standing at the wall of public phones for detainees, where every last one of them is in use, and with the men all speaking loudly.

"Probably trying to be heard through the static," Ahmed says jokingly, before switching gears and jumping into the case.

I'll discover across our six weeks with Esteban that Ahmed is as warm and gracious as he is focused and disciplined.

"Thanks for contacting us," he tells Esteban soberly. "I'd like to begin by asking you some questions, please."

Through his diligent questioning, he and I quickly learn that Esteban is a twenty-three-year-old mechanic from Havana and he's already been in detention in the United States for nearly three months.

We learn, too, that he crossed the border on foot through the Chihuahuan Desert between Mexico and the United States. There he'd wandered lost until being picked up by a US Border Patrol agent in a green uniform outside of Santa Teresa, New Mexico. It had been a scorching afternoon. Esteban remembers the brisk air conditioning inside the border agent's vehicle.

Esteban mentions, too, that he couldn't understand the agent, who spoke only the tiniest bit of broken Spanish.

He remembers that the agent drove him to a station, talked to him there almost indecipherably in front of a computer, and then had him transferred to a detention center, but not the one he's currently in.

It's crucial information for Ahmed, but it has come at a price. Our time together is limited, and it has taken most of an hour to gather that backstory. By his own admission, Esteban is a quiet, reserved person. He dislikes conversation, especially about himself. And here we are, strangers, on the phone, prodding him for intimate details of traumatic moments in his past.

Meanwhile, as he himself explained it, he likes being a mechanic because he enjoys the hours of uninterrupted solitude when working on the puzzle of a broken-down motor. Instead, he's standing at a busy wall of public phones in a detention center, having to answer private questions in public, and with his life in the balance as a refugee.

With time running out on our meeting, Ahmed has no choice but to indelicately cut directly to the heart of the matter.

"Esteban, why did you request an urgent conversation with me this afternoon?"

"Because tomorrow I have my final appearance with a judge."

For a moment, no one speaks. All I hear is static, loud and thick.

Ahmed seems to be processing the revelation in slow motion. I can only imagine what he's thinking: that he'll have less than twenty-four hours to prep and fight his first case and the stakes are high.

"Wait, what do you mean?" he finally manages.

"They told me I see the judge tomorrow. It's my last chance to present my case."

As sad as it sounds, I've seen this many times before. Extreme haste seems to be a weapon used against refugees in their cases.

This happens in part because the refugees are dehumanized by laws like Title 42 and MPP. They can also suffer from a legal process known as "expedited removal," which dates back to the 1996 Illegal Immigration Reform and Immigrant Responsibility Act and allows for noncitizens to be deported without a hearing.

Additionally, politicians and media members frequently malign and scapegoat migrating people and refugees, only adding to the conditions for their dehumanization. Fortunately, we can change this. Laws can be amended. Voting can bring different politicians into office. We can hold the media accountable. And we can address our lack of sensible and adequate infrastructure for ethically receiving and supporting migrating people and refugees.

In his sudden rush through legal proceedings after an indefinite wait in detention, Esteban's predicament reminds me of my work in Dilley. There, too, within a single afternoon, I'd sometimes meet a client, interview her, prepare her for her asylum interview, and see her off to the Asylum Office, only to find out hours later that she'd been scheduled for deportation after having failed to convince the government of her need for asylum due to credible fear of returning to her country of origin.

Typically, rushed clients bristle with anxious energy. Esteban, however, is calm. He's a gentle introvert who seems able to remain buoyant even in gale force winds on a nerve-wracking sea at night. And it's actually his attorney who seems a bit rattled, as evident by his eruption of rapid-fire legal questions for Esteban.

"So you've seen a judge before?" Ahmed asks Esteban.

"Yes, once. Well, twice."

"Once or twice?"

"Twice."

"What did the first judge discuss with you?"

"Why I crossed from Mexico into the United States."

"Did that judge give you any instructions about that?"

"Yes. I'm supposed to prepare the paperwork that he gave me for tomorrow."

"And do you have that paperwork?"

"Yes, but not on me. It's in my cell."

"Can you remember what it says?"

"No."

"Why not?"

"Because I don't know what it says. It's in English."

Everything is moving fast, except for the revelation of information, which is painfully slow and cryptic. And the clock is ticking on our time together.

"The hearing is tomorrow?"

"Yes."

I know we have mere minutes left on the call. My mouth is dry with the tension. I mute myself to clear my throat, hoping that Ahmed is an Olympic sprinter of lawyering.

"Can you remember what *kind* of paperwork the judge gave you?" Ahmed asks.

"To ask to live here, with asylum."

Ahmed pauses very briefly to think, then switches angles.

"Have you ever been interviewed by a US border agent?" he asks.

"I think so."

"What do you mean by that?" Ahmed asks patiently. "Can you tell me more?"

"Well, the man in green who picked me up in the desert asked me questions at the station, but, like I said, I didn't really understand him. Maybe he interviewed me?"

"What did you tell him?"

"That I'm Cuban."

"Anything else?"

"My name, my birthday."

"Anything else?"

I could hear stress tightening Ahmed's throat, his pitch rising ever so slightly. And why wouldn't it? How to work a case by phone for a desperate refugee with a court appearance in less than twenty-four hours?

"Why *did* you cross the border?" Ahmed asks, trying yet another approach.

"I want to live in the United States."

"For what reason?"

"Because in Cuba I was harassed for my political opinions."

And with that our time together is nearly done. Esteban has to relinquish the phone. Ahmed has other clients waiting. This was after all a last-minute arrangement for all of us.

In our final seconds, we hurriedly set an emergency meeting for tomorrow morning at 9:15 a.m. MST.

"Esteban, please try to bring the paperwork with you, if you can."

"I will, Mr. Ahmed," he says. "Thank you. And thank you, Mr. Seth."

And with that, we all hang up.

~~~~~~~

"Good morning, Seth," Ahmed says cheerily. "Thanks for making time between classes."

"My pleasure," I say, immediately regretting my choice of words, "pleasure" being all wrong here.

"Good news. We. . . ." But before he can finish, the operator cuts in.

"Stand by to be connected," and then that same static from yesterday.

"¿Hola?"

It's Esteban, but his voice again sounds distant, filtered, as if it's emerging from a deep underwater cave.

"Good morning, Esteban," Ahmed says warmly. "I have wonderful news. Your court appearance isn't today. It's in roughly three weeks. I was able to track down your ICE file."

"Thank you, Mr. Ahmed," Esteban replies, the relief audible in his tone. "Thank you. Thank you. I don't know what to say."

Esteban is surely dizzy with the news. He'd spoken of fearing being deported today if the hearing went poorly. Now this; he can breathe. He has time to work with his attorney. He might just win his case.

"Did you bring your paperwork?" Ahmed asks, ever focused and diligent.

"Yes."

"What does it say?"

"I don't know. I can't read much English."

"Well, what are the numbers or letters at the top of the page, maybe in an upper corner?"

Esteban spells out the titles and codes atop the forms, and Ahmed sighs with audible relief. He explains that those forms are standard, issued to everyone in detention, and that he'll download them later today from a government website and begin to complete them for Esteban.

"Thank you, Mr. Ahmed," Esteban says. "Thank you. Thank you."

But rather than celebrate this small relief, Ahmed pushes on. He is disciplined and hopeful. He lays out the legal plan he's devised for Esteban's case, which he hopes will help Esteban to cope with the humiliating degradations of life in detention between now and the court date.

"We'll meet regularly like this," Ahmed explains, "by phone, to prepare you for your hearing. I'll guide you step-by-step. I'm cautiously optimistic, though I can't promise anything. And I hope the plan makes sense. Do you have any questions?"

"No."

"Ok, then let's move on. There's a lot to do in little time, even with the three weeks."

"Yes, of course," Esteban replies, a new vigor to his voice, subtle but discernible.

And that's another thread in the fabric of heartbreak enveloping this case in particular and our immigration system in general. Esteban is tenderhearted, gentle, and gracious at every turn. Even when cornered, he doesn't snap or growl at us. He remains calm and helpful. And he's unassuming to the point that I wonder if it might hurt him in his court appearance.

Ahmed begins to explain that he needs certain documents and evidence from Esteban in order to fight the case. Almost immediately, we hit another potentially debilitating snag. A detainee must have a sponsor in the United States to be released.

Thankfully, Esteban is all set. He has one. It's his father-in-law's sister, Damasia, a Cuban refugee, living in Boston on a US green card. Ahmed explains that he'll need a copy of Damasia's permanent resident card, driver's license, most recent tax return, and a statement that declares that she's willing to serve as Esteban's sponsor. That sounds simple enough, but Esteban's court date is in three weeks, and Damasia is on vacation in Cuba for the next four weeks.

Ahmed goes silent at the news. I can't tell over the phone if he's clenching his jaw in frustration or if he's calmly brainstorming options for moving forward.

Apparently, it's the latter, because when he resumes speaking, he talks rapidly and fervently, proposing a detailed plan that's an all-out blitz on any and all avenues to secure those materials from Damasia in Cuba as quickly as possible.

Unfortunately, though, before he can finish, our allotted time for the phone call expires.

Before the call can cut out, Esteban quickly recites Damasia's WhatsApp number three times loudly through the static. While scribbling it down for Ahmed, I relay that we three will meet again in two days.

Over the next ten days, Esteban, Ahmed, and I meet four times by phone just to try to secure Damasia's correct contact information in both Cuba and Boston, and then to organize a plan for her documents to be sent to Ahmed.

That plan involves not only Damasia, but also her sister and husband in Cuba and her neighbor in Boston. Such is the practice of immigration law in the age of social media. One could say it takes a digital village for a refugee to receive the support he needs.

Amidst all that planning, one detail in particular strikes me: Ahmed has arranged for a prepaid courier to transport the documents to him from Damasia's neighbor in Boston. That meticulous and thoughtful attention to detail is a small but revealing act of Ahmed's character.

At the same time, Ahmed's act sends me spiraling into despair, concerned for the thousands of refugees without an attorney. Every last one of them should have a focused, thorough, thoughtful, well-resourced, and detail-oriented pro bono attorney.

So while it might seem frustratingly belabored, slow, and inefficient for it to take ten days of meetings, WhatsApp messages, phonecalls, texts, and email conversations among more than a half dozen people across the Americas for Esteban to deliver to Ahmed the basic materials that he needs, Esteban is, in fact, doing extremely well compared to the vast majority of detained refugees.

Moreover, the small minority of detainees like Esteban who are lucky enough to have attorneys are most often in that fortunate position due to the generosity of spirit of volunteers, whether strangers, family, neighbors, or friends.

"I can't represent you in the case," Ahmed is explaining to a crestfallen Esteban.

It's a cold and windy afternoon here in Charlottesville, and Esteban's hearing is in six days. I'm hurting for him. He's as stunned as he is baffled by the sudden, crushing news.

"What do you mean?" he asks, still in shock.

"I've just been informed by my supervisor that I can only represent you at a bond hearing, not in a master calendar case. That's the purview of my group."

Esteban still isn't understanding. Me, neither.

"And I can't represent you on my own because the courts require malpractice insurance for that, and I don't have it."

"I still don't understand."

"Please try not to worry," Ahmed offers empathetically, his voice pained and tight. "I reached out to a colleague about thirty minutes ago, and she agreed to represent you, if you'd like. But she doesn't work pro bono."

"What does that mean?" Esteben asks softly, still clearly reeling.

"It means you'd have to pay her. She's standing by, in case you're interested. I can patch her in, if you'd like. Her name is Amanda."

In Ahmed's mad scramble to secure a replacement attorney on such short notice, this was the best he could do. No one else he'd reached could even take on the case for pay, let alone pro bono, overburdened as immigration dockets and attorneys are these days.

"I guess," Esteban mumbles, sounding farther away than he's ever been.

"I'll dial her now," says Ahmed, and all falls silent but for the static.

"Hi, Esteban," a friendly woman's voice breaks in. "This is Amanda. How are you doing?"

She sounds supportive, but in his shock Esteban remains silent.

"I'm so sorry you're in this predicament," she continues. "But I can help, if you'd like. What do you think?"

"Yes," Esteban says almost whispering, and I wonder how many human beings have failed him along his terrible journey.

"Great," Amanda says. "I just need to ask you a few questions, if that's ok."

"Yes," he says, and I wince at the forthcoming experience for him: the tedium and frustration for a client in having to repeat a personal narrative replete with all of the retraumatizing triggers.

"When did you enter the United States?"

"About three months ago."

"Where did you enter?"

"The Chihuahuan Desert."

"What's your nationality?"

"Cuban."

"How old are you?"

"Twenty-three."

"Have you ever been interviewed by an agent of the US government?"

"I don't know."

"You don't know?"

"No."

"Ok. Why did you leave Cuba?"

"I was being harassed for my politics."

"What kind of work did you do?"

"Mechanic."

It goes on like this, with Esteban repeating his story yet again to another US person. Friend or foe, it must feel all the same to him by now, like he's running in place in quicksand, sinking deeper and deeper, finding it ever more difficult to breathe, and reaching out for a helping hand that's always made of sand too.

This is yet another problematic consequence of the current system: it leaves little room to protect the mental health of people who have suffered traumatic experience. To the contrary, they are compelled to repeat their traumatic stories gratuitously, over and over with little to no benefit to them.

"Mr. Seth," Esteban interrupts, breaking the artifice of interpreted conversation. "Please ask Mrs. Amanda how much it will cost to have her as my attorney."

"Amanda," I say. "Please forgive the interruption, but how much will it cost to represent the case?"

"Seeing as I can work with Ahmed through our office," she says, "I'll only charge for the master calendar case, which would be $1,500 for the appearance next week."

"Thank you," Esteban says, "but I'm sorry. I don't have that kind of money."

"No problem," says Amanda. "I understand."

"Thank you, Mrs. Amanda," he replies, ever gracious.

Amanda exits the conference call. Esteban, Ahmed, and I sit in an awkward silence until Ahmed is struck by an epiphany.

"I just thought of another colleague who might help!" he exclaims. "She sometimes even works pro bono. I'll reach out to her straight away."

"Thank you, Mr. Ahmed," Esteban says, a new thread of sadness laced in his voice. "And if that doesn't work, can you please help me to fill out my paperwork? It's in English."

"I'll do my best," Ahmed says. "But I don't think I can file it for you. I'll let you know for sure tomorrow morning."

And just like that, with the case suddenly haywire, our time is up for today.

~~~~~~

"Good news," Ahmed tells Esteban the following morning. "My colleague, Roberta, has agreed to represent you pro bono."

His conscience deeply troubled, Ahmed had spent the previous afternoon and evening reaching out to anyone and everyone whom he could think of in his legal circles to ask for help. This morning Roberta came through.

"Oh, thank you, Mr. Ahmed!" Esteban says, delighted, the emotional rollercoaster gathering speed again.

Esteban's voice radiates relief. I feel it through the line, and it's contagious, so much so that I find I'm smiling now as I interpret the conversation.

"Roberta is standing by to join us," Ahmed says. "If you'd like to meet her, then I'll patch her in."

"Yes, please."

"Good morning, Esteban," she says, materializing as if from nowhere. "This is Roberta. How are you doing?"

Her voice is pillowy and friendly, but she's all business. She dives right in. Again, it's the same procession of questions that Esteban has been through a million times before.

"What is your country of origin?"

"Cuba."

"How old are you?"

"Twenty-three."

"On what date did you enter the United States?"

"About three months ago."

"Where did you cross the border?"

"Through the Chihuahuan Desert."

"How did you end up in detention?"

"A US agent in green arrested me in the desert. He transferred me to his station, then to the first prison, then to here."

"Have you ever seen a judge in the United States?"

"Yes, on a video screen in the first detention center."

"What did he tell you?"

"I'm not sure."

"Did you receive an N.T.A., or Notice to Appear?"

"I don't know."

Ahmed interrupts.

"Roberta, it's Ahmed," he says. "I ordered a copy of the N.T.A. from ICE, and I'm waiting to receive it. I can share it when I do."

"Thanks, Ahmed," she responds, then returns to Esteban without missing a beat. "And, Esteban, what else did the judge say or do, if anything?"

"I don't know. It was hard to follow."

"Did you see him again?"

"No. I was supposed to, but they transferred me to Otero."

"Ok, no problem. Did you tell the first judge that you were afraid to return to Cuba?"

"No."

"Why not?"

"He didn't ask me about Cuba."

"What did he ask about?"

"He asked me about Mexico."

"What did you tell him?"

"That I didn't ever want to go back there, that it was horrible."

"Did he ask you why you entered the United States?"

"Yes."

"What did you tell him?"

"That I want to live here. I want asylum."

"How did he respond?"

"He gave me paperwork to complete for him."

"Did you complete it?"

"No, it was in English. And before I could figure out what to do, I was transferred to Otero."

"Ok, no problem. Did you see any other judges in the United States?"

"Yes, I saw one here, at Otero. This time he was in person, not on a screen."

"And what did you tell him?"

"I don't know. I was really nervous."

"Can you explain?"

"Well, I didn't have the paperwork ready from the other judge and thought I might get in trouble for that. So I kind of panicked. I remember feeling like it was hard to breathe."

"What did the judge say or do, if anything?"

"The judge was nice. He gave me extra time to do the paperwork. But I didn't understand what else he said. I thought I had a date in court, but it must've been something else. Like I said, I was nervous. I'm sorry."

"That's ok. No problem. Did you tell him anything else, maybe about your asylum petition, about your reasons for wanting to live here, in the United States?"

"I told him I was harassed in Cuba for my politics. I told him how I was bothered by police at work and at home, how they even talked to my sister and neighbors. And one time they roughed me up a little and said I could lose my job, go to jail, if I didn't change my ways."

Roberta pauses. It sounds like she's drawing in a deep breath through her teeth, then silence, static.

"Ok, Esteban," she finally resumes, "here is what I'm going to do: I'm going to try to get you out on bond in advance of your individual hearing."

"I don't understand," he says.

"I'm going to submit a bond packet for you, hopefully this afternoon, and by tomorrow afternoon at the latest. If we win, then you'll be allowed to leave the detention center and await your court date on the outside, not detained in Otero. Does that make sense?"

"Yes. Thank you, Mrs. Roberta. And thank you, Mr. Ahmed. Thank you, Mr. Seth."

"No need for thanks," she rejoins quickly. "Let's hope I can get you out on bond."

"Yes, of course."

"And, Esteban, even if it works, it will only get you out on bond for a couple of days before your hearing, but that's better than nothing, right? It's the best I can do."

"Yes, thank you, Mrs. Roberta," Esteban says.

"Ok, I'll be in touch, Esteban. Thank you. Take good care."

"Thank you, Mrs. Roberta. Thank you, Mr. Ahmed. Thank you, Mr. Seth. Thank you. Thank you."

~~~~~~

Two days later, Ahmed and I are back on the phone with Esteban, at his request because he hasn't heard from Roberta.

"I apologize for that," Ahmed says. "I've just heard from her myself."

"Thank you, Mr. Ahmed."

"Don't thank me yet. I'm afraid it's not good news. Thirty minutes ago the judge denied our bond request. He thinks you're a flight risk."

"What does that mean?"

"It means you have to stay in Otero until your individual hearing, where Roberta will represent you."

"Why?"

"Because the judge thinks that if he lets you out on bond, you'll run off, disappear."

"Why would he think that of me? I promise not to. I'm responsible."

That is in fact a statistical truth of most people seeking asylum. When represented by an attorney, between 96 percent and 99 percent of asylum-seeking adults on bond make their court dates, and 99 percent of children do.[2]

"I know," Ahmed says. "Trust me. I believe you. And I'm sorry. Try to stay positive. You have your individual hearing coming up, and Roberta's a very good attorney."

"Yes, Mr. Ahmed. Thank you."

~~~~~~

Three days later, I'm trundling into my house through the garage door with Joaquín. It's 8:45 p.m. We're just home from his evening soccer practice, and we're joking around, swapping funny ideas about what to make for dinner.

"Peanut-butter cupcake casserole with pickled radish?" I suggest.

"No," he replies, laughing. "Frog-tongue tacos with cotton-candy ice cream as salsa."

Joaquín heads upstairs to shower, and I hit the kitchen pantry to grab a box of spaghetti. Just as I'm setting the pot of water to boil, my phone rings.

Normally I'd ignore it. Today I taught three classes, held office hours, led a meeting, and coached a soccer practice. I'm tired of speaking, and I have the raw throat to prove it. Plus, I need to cook quickly so that my sons can get to bed at a reasonable hour on a school night.

But I've been waiting on pins and needles for any news of Esteban's case, so I look at my phone and am glad I did. It's Ahmed. I always pick up for him, any day, any hour.

"Hi, Ahmed."

"Good evening, Seth. Sorry to call after hours East Coast time, but I have news from New Mexico. Do you have a minute?"

"I do. Thanks for calling. What's the news?"

"The judge just heard Esteban's case, and I'm sorry to say it didn't go our way."

My heart sinks, a stone thrown hard into the sea and plunging into deepening darkness.

"What happened?" I ask, my head spinning.

"The judge wasn't convinced of our arguments. He doesn't believe there are grounds for credible fear."

"I don't understand."

"He thinks Esteban can return safely to Cuba. He said if there were a pressing fear, then Esteban would've mentioned it to the first judge that interviewed him."

"That's absurd," I exclaim, more stridently than I would've wished. "That judge didn't *ask* Esteban about Cuba. That's why he didn't mention it. How is that his fault? He answered what he was asked."

"I know, but today's judge saw that discrepancy between the interviews as a flaw in Esteban's case, so we lost."

"What does that mean for Esteban now?"

"He's been scheduled for deportation, likely by early next week."

~~~~~

CHAPTER 7

Matamoros Again and Again

You must be able to see the world and go to it.

— ALFRED DÖBLIN

Another dawn in the Matamoros refugee camp, and again it's cold, the sky pale gray. And again, I'm walking alone through this grim expanse of tents.

I'm following a dirt path strewn with litter, the sun barely peeking out. Shadows enhance the sense of this place as a real-life dystopian neighborhood. I ignore the sadness building in my belly and allow myself to be carried along by the scent of burning mesquite.

The first fires of the day have just been lit. The air smells sweet and woody. It's so pleasant it almost delights me. I say "almost" because there's no delight here; that smell emanates from desperate flames. Lost in thought about the many agonies here, I drift from the maze of tents into a small clearing.

It's an internal oasis within the camp, and an aluminum trailer sparkles at its center. Across the back of the trailer, red block letters declare MOBILE MEDICAL UNIT. It's the new and only venue here for healthcare, run by Global Response

Management (GRM), who arrived only last month but set quickly to work.

This morning, two GRM doctors are already buzzing about the trailer. They're prepping for what's sure to be another busy shift. This camp of thousands is flush with sick people. Both doctors are women, in their forties or fifties, and they sport warm jackets and hats against the cold and wind.

Noticing me, they pause to say hello, and we fall easily into friendly conversation. They say they're from the States, here as volunteers. They've just been briefed that there are now close to four thousand refugees in camp due to the latest surge in numbers.

They tell me, too, that they expect today to treat mostly the flu. It's running through the camp, which they find medically unsurprising. Flu is typical this time of year, and it spreads more quickly in populations with few opportunities to maintain nutrition, access masks, wash hands, use tissues, and avoid close contact with others as much as possible, and especially with visibly sick people.

They add that those challenges are compounded here in the camp by people's nearly constant exposure to winter cold, not to mention the overwhelming stress of being a refugee. All of that combines to make it hard for people to stay healthy here and, if ill, to recover.

Still, the doctors say they're hopeful. They think they can bring the flu under control. They likewise think they can get a handle on the current outbreaks of lice and chicken pox. They say they're already making good headway on all three fronts.

What's much harder to treat, they say, are the many patients here who've survived violent trauma. For those patients, these doctors wish they had more resources and specialists, including social workers, psychologists, and psychiatrists.

More broadly, the doctors are troubled, too, by the general conditions here. The camp is massive, dirty, dangerous, and crowded, and their trailer is such a tiny help relative to the massive need.

Thankfully, the refugees are great patients: they're fastidiously compliant with doctor's orders, helping them to recover more quickly. And they're gracious during visits, even amidst all of their pain, stress, fear, cold, and hunger.

For these reasons and more, the doctors say they deeply appreciate this opportunity to serve this community. They mention, too, that they're here for a week but wish they could stay much longer. As it is, though, they're already exhausting their personal vacation days from their jobs in hospitals back in the States. In other words, these two doctors are here during their annual recess from their stressful jobs at busy hospitals. This is their vacation.

Their generosity inspires me. If everyone were to spend their vacations helping others, then the world would be a kinder place. In the case of these two doctors, they'll return to their respective hospitals as changed by their work here as their patients here have been.

All of this makes me think of my wife, also a physician, back home in rural Virginia. She's working overtime at her understaffed hospital, a regional trauma center serving a vast expanse of impoverished people. Therein she works in the hospital's emergency department, which is always busy. Many a shift she'll work eight to ten hours straight before even having a moment to herself to pee.

Making the shifts tougher still, the hospital is located in a region of the United States that's rife with white supremacists. This includes Neo-Confederates, white nationalists, and even chapters of the Ku Klux Klan. All of which are growing—in the twenty-first century.

Consequently, my wife, a Spanish-speaking, feminist immigrant from Latin America, is constantly saving the lives of people with odious ideas about humanity, and they frequently beg her help while wearing clothing decorated with Confederate flags and slogans. Under the clothing, their bodies sport Confederate tattoos, and even swastika tattoos.

And while she's slogging through her cases there this week, I missed her birthday to be here. At her urging. She insisted I make this trip. She supports my work on immigration reform, and she understands this is my chance to be here, given it's the winter break between my semesters of teaching at my home university.

So here I am, talking with these two inspirational doctors and thinking of a third. I'm remembering how my wife arrived in the States with little English in a cash-strapped family of five. And I'm recalling how very hard she's worked to overcome discrimination (and all the related hardships), in the States and become a full partner—the first woman in her group of emergency doctors. I think about how they save thousands of patients' lives each year, even if they're raging racists.

Speaking of patients, I know these two GRM doctors will soon be busy with them. I politely curtail our conversation and wish them well with their crucial work here.

Turning to leave, I discover two young girls are already sitting in the outdoor waiting room, which comprises little more than a folding table in front of a row of plastic chairs.

I smile at the girls, and I ask if I can talk with them. They say sure, and I sit down with them. I learn they're Daisy and Juanita, sisters, ages nine and five, respectively. Daisy, who's older, explains that they both have runny noses and pounding headaches, and that their mother told them to sit here and behave while she searches the camp for food. They're to wait right here, in these chairs, and talk to the doctor.

"Are you him?" Daisy asks me.

"No," I say. "The doctors are those two women in the trailer, and they're very nice."

I ask the girls if they're hungry, knowing my question to be rhetorical here, and when they nod yes, I quickly look around to see if anyone is watching us. With the coast clear, I furtively slide two granola bars from my backpack and give one to each child. I say "furtively" because hunger is everywhere here, and everywhere you're watched, especially if you're from the United States.

A friend of mine who lives in Brownsville and volunteers here regularly with the Angry Tías and Abuelas gave me a special admonition about food. She told me to be especially discreet whenever handing it out. Otherwise, I was likely to be swarmed by hungry people and cause quite a disturbance, however unintentionally.

In this case, though, all is copacetic. No one around seems to notice us, and no one appears. I watch Daisy tear open her granola bar packet in peace and pass it swiftly to her little sister. Daisy then tears open Juanita's bar, but before taking a bite, Daisy smiles at her sister and encourages her to eat, however strange the food.

Soon both girls are happily crunching on the bars and as we sit in silence. I smile in a kind of equanimity inspired by Daisy's compassionate care for her sister: even famished and sick, and young as she is, she took the time to attend to Juanita's needs before her own. What a beautiful person. And such grace resides in all of us, even if too often it remains latent.

With much to do, I have to keep moving. I rise to say goodbye to the girls and wish them a fast recovery. And as we wave goodbye to one another, I can't help but notice the grime on their palms and fingers. Hygiene is a huge problem here. There's little running water, aside from a line of six or eight spigots at a communal sink. Thankfully, some large water tanks have recently been delivered to the camp, but they're yet to be operational.

In the meantime, it's a constant struggle to stay clean. I've in fact given up on trying by day. Whatever I do wash myself in the morning, by midafternoon I seem to find myself coated in a sticky layer of rust-colored dust. And it clings not only to my body, but also to my clothes, backpack, hat, and boots. It makes me feel like I've been glazed in dirt, both inside and out. My eyes itch with the persistent dust, and I taste it on my tongue and in my throat. And I'm one of the extraordinarily lucky people here. Each night I go to my motel room, with its locking door and hot shower.

Each night in my motel room, I enjoy the incredible luxury of that shower. I stand in it naked yet safe, watching dirty water run off my body in thick, brown ropes. Simultaneously, I aggressively scrape not only every inch of my skin, but also the insides I can reach: my dust-clogged nostrils and ear canals, and the underside of each of my fingernails. Even more opulently, I have a treasure trove of accoutrements: I have cotton swabs, washcloths, towels, and abundant soap. I have shampoo and conditioner. I have toothpaste, floss, and a toothbrush with clean bristles.

Scrubbed and dried, I lie down in fresh clothes on a soft mattress covered in clean sheets to go to sleep. Snug between clean, white bedding and a clean, fluffy blanket, I nestle my tired head into a clean, soft pillow. The room is locked, safe, and warm. All around me, the night is quiet and tranquil. Who knew life in a cheap motel could be so decadent, so refreshing, so indulgent.

It's my final afternoon here, late in the day now, and the waning light has gone golden. And yet again by wandering this camp, I've met an amazing human being who's trapped here.

His name is José Luis. We're standing side by side at the northern edge of the camp, pressed right up against the border fence—kilometer zero.

"I know how to cook," he tells me with a quiet smile, looking down at the fire beneath him.

He's using a scrap of cardboard as a makeshift spatula to stir chicken skin in a pot of yellow, bubbling oil.

José Luis clearly delights in the cookery while explaining to me how delicious this dinner will be. The scraps of skin were a stunning gift from a friend who'd found work this morning and actually gotten paid for it. In joyful celebration, she bought the bird, boiled it in river water, and fed it to her family. But she saved the raw skin for José Luis, in gratitude for his help over the past week with her two sick, young children.

José Luis has no spices or herbs, no condiments or other ingredients. His recipe is simple: oil and chicken skin.

He got the oil from another friend whom he'd helped to get a tent. And he'd found the aluminum pot on a trash heap, which amounted to a mini dump.

The pot was badly dented, and its handle seemed to have snapped off long ago, leaving a sharp, plastic nub. But to José Luis, an accomplished cook, it was all he needed, and it seems to be doing the trick.

He has it balanced just so atop a fire of bundled sticks from a nearby copse of trees. The oil is roiling, and the skin is frying away in it, giving off a delicious aroma that draws neighbors in. He tells them time and again that the chicharrónes are not yet ready, but he'll share whatever he can when they're cooked.

Though he's been here for but three weeks, he's already well established socially. He explains that despite the massive size of the bloated camp, and the generalized atmosphere of fear, he's managed to find a niche and settle in, even making friends. He begins to proudly detail for me each of their names and the locations and colors of their tents, should I care to meet them, too, because they're all good people.

As José Luis talks, he gestures in the air with a dazzlingly eloquent left hand, like an orchestra conductor. Meanwhile his right hand is robotic: steadily swirling the chicken skin in its boiling oil.

He's twenty-eight, and slim and fit, with bulbous biceps and a powerful handshake.

He's wearing a T-shirt with the Stars and Stripes on it, and he tells me how much he's dreamed of opening a restaurant in the United States. It's where he's long hoped to live happily and freely with his small family of a wife and young daughter. They're soon to follow him along this route. Their plan is for him to settle in the States first and then to help them to make the trip more safely than he did.

"Back home, I had a café, pigs, a cow for milk," he explains. "I loved cooking for people and being with my family, especially my five-year-old daughter, who loves the kitchen too."

In the dying light of the winter afternoon, he goes silent. I imagine it must be the memory of his daughter. I think of my sons, home with my wife. Beneath us the fire pops and hisses.

We stare out in silence like this at the southern border of the United States. It's but a stone's throw from where we stand, a distance so short he could cross it in seconds, were it permitted.

But it's not. José Luis is trapped here by MPP. And I'm struck by the importance of a piece of paper to human well-being. All I need to do to cross the border into the States is flash my small, blue US passport at a CBP agent. The importance of paper. José Luis has an NTA from CBP with a court date of February 20, 2020. That's more than two months away. And when will he see his wife and daughter?

I break the silence.

"I'm sorry you have such a long wait here," I say, looking down with shame and toeing the dirt.

We stand again in silence. I've found such quiet to be common in the camp when pain eclipses language.

I glance furtively at José Luis, and by the last light of the day, I see his face is tight with feeling. To respect his privacy, I look quickly away, stare at the pot, watch the twists of skin crackle and spin in the bubbling oil.

And I marvel at the strength, courage, and ingenuity of this person, any person, still standing in this camp, weathering its hunger and cold, enduring the punishing wait for a court date.

This after José Luis has risked a perilous journey to save his life, to save his family. Only to be pinned here in a desperate, dangerous refugee camp, a few feet from his dream destination, which he's statistically unlikely ever to reach.

He breaks the silence by sharing the event that galvanized his journey here: he was arrested for vagrancy while searching for work in the capital. He'd been beaten with a nightstick, cited with a misdemeanor, and given a court date. Fearing incarceration, he decided it was his time to migrate. He tells me how he kissed his daughter goodbye before leaving secretly for the United States, and how much he's missed her since his lips left her cheek.

He first traveled to Panama. There he organized his trek to the US border, where we now stand, his dream suspended in place. He remains hopeful, though, of crossing and changing his family's future. He remains hopeful of opening a café in the

United States, where he'll make people happy with his cooking and where his daughter will love going to school.

He skims the finished *chicharrónes* from the oil with his cardboard spatula. The sight of the sparkling, crunchy skin seems to hearten him.

"I miss my daughter," he says abruptly. "I miss my mom, my wife, and my café. I loved to cook each day, make people happy, milk my cow, tend to my pigs."

Again the silence. Life is like this here: a flash of happiness swallowed quickly by the surrounding grief.

José Luis wipes a drip from his nose with two fingers. He apologizes, saying he's had a head cold for more than a week. I wonder if it's the flu that's running through the camp. Or maybe it's the cold that his friend's children had, making it the cost of this dinner. Or maybe it's just the stress of life here has run him down, or it's a reaction to the grit of life here, the grimy dust that coats us, the greasy smoke that streaks the air here from all the burning mesquite. Whatever it is, he ignores it, preoccupied by bigger concerns.

"The government took too much from me," he says cryptically.

I ask gently if he'll explain.

"I had to pay 65 percent of my net income to the government, and they watched my till on my café counter. People in the neighborhood had been assigned to it. They'd come by often and ensure they got at least that 65 percent. How could I make a living? At best I'd break even, and we were hungry, and we weren't free. No one can talk politics. If we were to talk like this, like you and I are doing, we'd both go to prison."

Again the silence.

By now it's dark, and the lights of the US border station blaze like an extravagant white fire. It's the burning threshold that José Luis hopes one day to cross and enter freedom.

For now, though, his dream of opening a café hovers like a mirage before a parched wanderer in a desert.

"I'd like to see Las Vegas," he adds, again flashing that sweet smile of his at me. I can see a sparkle of hope in his eyes as he imagines the trip.

Ever the host, the restaurateur, he offers me some of the fresh chicharrones. I politely decline, wanting every last calorie to go to him. And I'm deeply touched by his kindness. He'd share his dinner with me, a stranger, despite the hardship and desperation of his life here.

It's 38 degrees Fahrenheit and getting colder. He has no jacket, and he refuses mine when I offer it to him as a gift.

We stand again in that silence. A statistic comes to me, and I wince. Last month less than 1 percent of all refugees seeking asylum in the United States were granted it. That includes MPP cases.

And here we stand. At the very border. Kilometer zero. We're side by side, but worlds apart. How unjustly we judge and treat one another.

It's getting colder. Night is settling in. I watch José Luis shiver in the dying glow of his small fire, its pile of sticks now mostly ash.

~~~~~~

CHAPTER 8

Karla Has a Headache

How can we know the dancer from the dance?

— WILLIAM BUTLER YEATS

Karla has a headache. Again. Just like last week, her first in here. And just like last week, her head is down, pegged forehead-first to the cold steel table.

She's been like that, unmoving, since I first walked into the cellblock this morning for our weekly poetry workshop. Upon seeing her, I was immediately concerned. A paternal alarm was sounding in my belly, the kind that told me to worry over my children when they were injured during a soccer game, or when they were very sick in bed in the morning, feverish, and needed to miss school.

"*¿Estás bien?*" I asked gently, pausing next to her at the table.

"*Sí*," she replied softly, but I knew she wasn't.

I could hear the hurt in her raspy voice. It sounded tight and thin, like a blue thread stretched taut to the point of snapping, then held there, trembling, hypertense.

My stomach soured. I wanted to sit down and talk with her, but there was neither privacy nor time for it.

A dozen other children and two guards had all fallen silent, watching me navigate my entrance to the room. They were as eager to note how I made my way past Karla as they were for me to begin our workshop, our time together always all too brief.

To mask my concern for Karla and connect with the other children, I looked out at them and forced a casual smile. I walked my way deeper into the cellblock, wanting to pull everyone's focus away from Karla, slumped in private pain at her table, alone.

I'd learned long ago through my work in prisons that few challenges are more difficult for imprisoned people than dealing with pain in public spaces. In places like this, pain is a vulnerability, and vulnerability is dangerous. It exposes the pained person to all sorts of social pressure, and it opens them to the risk of manipulation and coercion and violence, from both the guards and from fellow incarcerated people. All of this in turn exacerbates the sufferer's sense of loneliness and isolation, which is often what they are struggling with in the first place.

Making things tougher still for Karla, she was new to this facility, and she was currently the only girl in the workshop on this cellblock. So she was uniquely vulnerable, uniquely exposed, and she was uniquely disoriented and alone. I knew I had to be exceptionally delicate in any attempt to work with her, especially in front of others. That's why I'd moved away from her so quickly despite my concern for her. I simultaneously made a mental note for myself to get back to her discreetly, and as soon as possible, for a safe-space conversation.

Such are the complexities of running a poetry workshop in a detention center or prison.

Besides the constant pressure to maintain institutional policies in relation to the collective needs and pain of the incarcerated people comprising each workshop on each cell-block, there exists an acute pressure to balance the individual needs and troubles of each participant with those of their peers. Accordingly, I worried constantly over how best to listen to and for each child specifically, and, consequently, how to create an individuated, private, welcoming, and safe space for each of them.

In this manner, I hoped to coordinate the conditions for vibrant, trusting connections to be made among these vulnerable children as an active and open community of poets. And all this despite our being continuously surveilled by guards ambling among us with their chirping radios and video cameras on the walls above us, recording our every action, gesture, and utterance.

And here I am, standing in the center of all of this on the cellblock this morning. Privately, I worry about Karla while publicly explaining the theme for the workshop today: reading and writing poetry about ways of dealing with discrimination.

Overall, my hopes are high that the day will prove fruitful. I'm surrounded by these fabulous young poets. They are bright and eager to share. And although they frequently detail in writing and conversation the ways that vicious iterations of discrimination have deeply hurt them, they are nevertheless ebullient with big dreams for the future. They focus on starting careers and families while living happily, safely, and freely in the States.

Such talk, in fact, peppers my every visit. And today is no different. I can sense in the air how they're bristling with energy, like sprinters in their starting blocks, legs twitching. Each child seems ready to write, share, and listen. Except Karla. Her head is still down. Her body is still motionless.

141

From a table by the guards' station, Juan Carlos shoots up his hand and leaves it there emphatically moving. He's an impulsive, hyper child, and I'm worried he's going to ask about Karla or, worse, ask her something directly, in front of everybody. Instead, he asks me sweetly what the weather is like outside this morning. I breathe a sigh of relief and smile at him.

It's a common question in here, and one that never ceases to break my heart. Because the children here aren't allowed outside, something they lament to me in writing and in conversation. They write of running outside on beaches and in pastures and on soccer fields shining bright with sunlight. In reality, the only natural light they know filters in through thin windows high up on the far wall of the cellblock. I often imagine that light as slicing in above our heads like the thin sheet of ice atop a frozen lake, beneath which the children hold their breath, looking up, treading water, and trying not to freeze.

Samuel cuts in. He's a jubilant, impatient child with a thick Honduran accent. He asks how my family is doing. I tell him they're fine, and he nods happily, appeased by the news. It's because he knows and likes my wife, having met her in the emergency room where she works one frigid night a few months back. He'd tried to kill himself, and she'd been the doctor to treat him. He told me all about it in our next workshop. I remember noticing how his body was still visibly scarred from the episode, and I remember noting his exceptional tenderness, something that surely makes life in here all the more punishing for him. He spoke of how kind my wife had been to him that night; how she'd bandaged his wrists so gently; and how she'd talked him through everything in Spanish, the only Spanish-speaker in the entire ER.

At some point, he'd told her that one way he tries to cope with his depression is by writing poetry about it in the detention center. That led my wife and him to realize that *el poeta* with whom he attended the workshops there was none other than her husband. Ever since, he's asked me regularly for updates on her well-being.

A few more children want to interact personally with me, too, as we reconnect after a week apart. We take turns exchanging warm and genuine greetings and tiny bits of news. The children seem to delight in the interaction, and I do, too, smiling affectionately into each child's face and reminding each and every one of them that I care about them, as do many people beyond the facility.

All the while, though, my mind remains split. One half is sunny and enthused by all the love that the children are conjuring. But the other half remains dark and stormy with a deep concern for Karla, the newest person trapped in here, and seemingly struggling mightily.

And how could I *not* worry about Karla specifically? Here she was, freshly locked up here, in this disorienting, white-washed concrete building that could be anywhere, and was most certainly far from any potential family and any familiar culture. And she was living in an isolation cell, compounding her sense of dislocation from humanity, from community.

I certainly worry for all of these children for those reasons. The lived conditions herein are brutal by design as a mechanism to combat immigration to the United States. My nation has been wrongheaded in determining incarceration to be a primary tool for confronting the global reality of mass migration due to climate change, economic inequality, and political corruption.

On a more granular level, here on the ground in the detention center, it's well-documented that isolation harms the human mind. So its use in carceral facilities cannot be understood as anything other than intentionally violent, not to mention cruel and unusual punishment. And like the deprivation of sunlight, the children write and talk regularly about how much they're suffering from the brutalizing solitude of their lives in here.

On top of all this, there's also an acute and individual urgency to my worry for Karla. It's because of the pain in her voice, because of her second consecutive disabling headache, and because of the way her head was unnaturally planted face-first on the cold steel table—unmoving.

To get back to her as soon as feasible, I tweak my plan for the workshop today, quickly reordering its components. I pull out our poem for the day and solicit two volunteers to read it aloud. It's titled "I, Too," by Langston Hughes, and I contextualize it briefly before we hear the two readings. I explain that it's a poem written by a masterful writer of the Harlem Renaissance. The poem speaks to fighting for Black arts and rights and protesting racism. I add that it was first published when the poet was barely twenty-four years old, making him only a few years older than the group.

Multiple children have raised their hands to volunteer to read it, and I take advantage of their hyperattention in the moment to explain a few further, prefatory aims for our work today through this poem. First and foremost, I ask the children to listen for any strong feelings that might emerge from the poem, reminding them that they, too, want to conjure strong feelings with their own writing. Second, I ask them to note any striking images or actions in the poem, and how they affect the narrative. Third, I ask a formal question: how does Hughes use repetition in the poem? Fourth and finally, I ask the children to listen for any differences between the two forthcoming readings by their peer volunteers.

We've long discussed that there is much pleasure to be had in reading aloud. It's artful, expressive work. It's something to be enjoyed and savored, by both audience and reader, who are sometimes one and the same, as when they're alone in their cells.

All the while, I glance sporadically at Karla, who's yet to move. She still has her face down, still has her hands on her nape with her fingers interlaced there. It makes her look as if some phantom wrestler, invisible but for his hands, were pinning her face-first to the mat sadistically. And I'll soon learn that she *is* in fact wrestling, with both a headache and a phantom.

For now, though, we're all listening to Edwin slowly read aloud "I, Too." A sweet and sensitive seventeen-year-old from El Salvador, he reads with a striking, dramatic passion. His pace is slow and deliberate, as I've been encouraging of the children in our every workshop to do. And Edwin excels at it. He has the soul of an artist and the rich baritone of an elegant radio host.

But his aesthetic interests aren't oratorical, but culinary. He hopes to become a celebrated chef here in the States. I'm confident that he can do it, if given the chance. He's not only creative, hardworking, and resourceful, but also detail-oriented, self-confident, and generous.

When Edwin finishes his reading, it's Manuel's turn. A curly-haired jokester from El Salvador, he begins his turn by singing out a few notes, making us laugh. He then begins again, this time soberly, and like Edwin, he reads the poem earnestly and delicately. It reminds me that these children are some of the best students of poetry with whom I've worked. They listen carefully to every voice, whether in conversation or writing, and they apply what they learn quickly, writing better poem by poem.

While listening to Manuel, I edge my way back towards Karla. By the time he's finished, I'm standing beside her. We all applaud Manuel's fine reading, except for Karla. I ask the children to write now in response to hearing "I, Too."

My request surprises them. Typically, we'll discuss a poem as a whole group after hearing it read aloud to us by two children, and before jumping into individual writing, or writing in pairs or small groups. But today is different, I explain. I'd like them to hold all of their comments, questions, and confusions about the poem for now, and to channel all of that frustrated conversation into their individual writing. I tell them more broadly that they can do this anytime, with any frustration, whether it be over the food in here or over missing their family or over an interaction with a friend or guard or over their court cases. I tell them that to write like this can be soothing. It can help them to work through complex, painful feelings, especially venomous ones. I add, too, that we'll soon discuss their comments, confusions, and questions about the poem. I'd simply like them to write for a bit first.

Such is our process. Each workshop is a blend of reading, talking, writing, and sharing. The order sometimes varies, but they know and thrive within the general schema. At least in part, it works well because they helped to design it. That is, from the start we together have devised the system by which we work, and we keep refining it to suit our changing needs. That democratic spirit of our shared experience has helped us immeasurably to cohere as a group. We've come together as a mutually supportive and active community of poets with surprising fluidity.

Consequently, each child plays an important, dignifying role in the orchestration of our time together. This grants them something adjacent to control over themselves, and over their experience in here, where almost everything else is bluntly dictated to them by institutional authority. So their autonomy and voice in workshop matter deeply to them, well beyond any discussion of any individual poem. Certainly, that reclaimed agency is temporary, lasting as it does for the duration of a workshop. Still, though, it matters. It's a glint of hope, normalcy, and self-affirmation in an otherwise desolate landscape of bleak subordination and censorship.

Nor do I mean to deny my privilege and authority in the group. I'm well aware always that I stand explicitly and implicitly before them as the adult leader of our workshops, meaning here that I'm sanctioned by the power of the detention center's top administrators. Thus, I function as an extension of their system, their infrastructure, the one oppressing the children. Plus, I'm an extensively published poet and longstanding teacher, which only adds to my inevitable authority over and distance from these children in our workshops.

To try to negotiate that power differential in ways helping the children and behooving good writing, I aspire consciously throughout each workshop to empower them. I do this in a multitude of ways, though most comprise some variety of either celebrating their achievements and/or ceding my control of the group to them. This includes my conscious efforts to let them direct conversations, to define literary excellence, and to attend to their writing slowly and attentively, according to their interests and feedback for one another. Besides helping the children, this transforms the space in which we meet.

That is, by coming together as self-directing poets who follow our own, self-determined rules of comportment in this space, we tinker with the typical function of the cellblock. We bump up against its limits. We temporarily disrupt and repurpose its designed function. The children change it from a punitive prison to an artists' studio, even if only temporarily and fractionally. Their lived violence never ceases, but it can be held at bay for brief moments. We can take a radical joy in being together through writing. The children can celebrate themselves in all of their wondrous differences, even if the site is designed to contain, control, shame, punish, stereotype, and censor them. More practically, still, every second spent writing and discussing literature is a second not spent despairing in being alone, self-harming, or attempting suicide.

Like right now. It's time for individual writing. That also makes it my chance to try to talk with Karla. Throughout the cellblock, all I can hear is the scritch of the children's two-inch rubber pens flying across the pages of their writing journals, and the odd beep or staticky conversation coming from the guards' radios.

I slide into a seat beside Karla. She's otherwise alone at her table because of the gendered rules of the detention center. They prefer to separate girls from boys in the workshop. She also lives in a separate cellblock, for girls, though there are few here in the detention center at the moment. Of the three or four of them, she alone has been assigned to this male cellblock for her workshop time. The boys have been eager to welcome her into the group, though she's yet to participate. She's hardly even moved. I've never had a child respond like this in here.

All of her stillness and all of her silence add to the sense that she's lost in private pain. I want to respect her need for privacy, her self-protection and self-seclusion, but something also urges me to intrude. Maybe it's because I know she has few opportunities in here to connect with others in the way we do in workshop, and every one of them is precious. Or maybe it's because I grew up in chronic pain myself, due to a hip disease. I spent much of my youth on hand crutches, in a wheelchair, sleeping in traction, and having surgery. I acutely remember what it was like to be a child trapped in pain and alone, separated from my peers socially, physically, and emotionally. I don't want Karla to suffer alone in here. Or maybe it's because I'm a teacher now, and I take seriously the calling's charge of engaging all students and trying to nurture them. Or maybe it's because I'm a parent, and by now I've learned ways to notice, acknowledge, and soothe some of the pain in children.

Whatever the reasons, I'm impelled to reach out to Karla. I begin by asking again if she's ok. When she doesn't answer this time, we sit together in silence. I learned long ago to respect such silence, both in prisons and in children. Karla remains utterly still, and I simply wait, trying not to move either. I just sit there with her in a kind of solidarity. Then slowly, unexpectedly, she swivels her face ever so slightly towards me until I see one hazel eye staring out at me over her bicep. Other than that slow roll of her face towards me, her body still hasn't moved, but I watch her blink, in silence. I smile at her softly and hold our eye contact. I can tell she's sizing me up, wondering if she can trust me.

When she finally speaks, I can barely hear her. Her voice has dropped to a strained whisper. I can't tell if it's because her headache has worsened or if she's meaning to match the quieted room. I assume it's both and lean in, but not too close, wanting to respect her space and body. I don't want to scare her back into silence by seeming too eager. Nor do I want to be reprimanded by the lurking guards for being too close to a detained person. So there I wait, ever so gently present in the inches of space between our faces, hoping she'll trust me as an ally, though she has little to no reason to. To her immense credit as a person of courage and truth, she takes a deep breath, then shares her story, teaching me a lesson about strength and resilience.

She begins by taking me back to a fateful Sunday morning in Soyapango, San Salvador, where she was born and raised in a small apartment with her grandma and mother. That morning, her beloved *abuela* had sent her out to buy a chicken from the market. She'd needed an extra bird for their family brunch, which would be later that afternoon. Karla's *Tío* Elber had just called to say his brother and he were coming over for the weekly family meal, and each man was bringing his new girlfriend.

Karla had been excited. She always loved it when her *tíos* visited, and she was eager to meet their girlfriends. She'd heard much about them, or as much as she could squeeze from her two tightlipped *tíos*.

So out she'd trotted on her errand, delighted by the excursion. She felt so lucky that morning: it was Sunday, meaning no school; she had money in her pocket to buy food; it was sunny and warm; and her grandma was cooking chicken and rice, her favorite meal, which she'd enjoy with her *tíos* and meet their girlfriends.

As she walked, carefree, Karla had no idea her life was about to change forever. Like most teens, she couldn't imagine how a couple of seconds could alter the entirety of her earthly existence. Because she hadn't yet run into Desastre that morning. Because she had no idea he'd even been released from prison. Because she'd forgotten how he'd always lusted after her, even way back when she was a timid thirteen-year-old and he was a street savvy eighteen- or nineteen-year-old.

She was now but a few blocks from the market, lost in thought, daydreaming about colors of lipstick. She was hoping to buy a new shade on her way back home if she had enough change after purchasing the chicken. And it was then, while she was deliberating between glossy cherry red and dark carmine in her head, that Desastre emerged. It was as if he'd materialized from nowhere and blocked her path down the sidewalk, like a storm cloud formed just for her.

"Daaamn, girl," he said, grinning like a hungry wolf. "You lookin' good. All grown and shit."

"Excuse me," she replied, trying to sidestep him, but he mirrored her movement.

"What's your rush, girl? Don't you like me?"

"I'm in a hurry," she said curtly.

She looked down and tried to push past him. The next thing she knew, he'd clapped a hand over her mouth and was dragging her into the alley.

As she twisted and flailed, she felt a hand slither up under her skirt. Instinct kicked in, and she bit down, hard, on that hand that was smothering her.

Desastre let out a scream and released her. She remembers him cursing and waving around his bleeding hand. Then there was a boom and all went black.

Karla pauses her story to scan the cellblock around us for interlopers, not wanting to be overheard. Reassured of our relative privacy, she quietly continues.

"Desastre had shot me in the head," she tells me, looking me dead in the eye.

Her grandma says she was saved by angels. Her mom says it was *la Virgen de Guadalupe*. The doctors said they could hardly believe Karla's good fortune in pulling through.

She explains to me that she's still deaf in one ear and has ringing in the other, and she still suffers chronic headaches and bouts of dizzying nausea. She says the planned suite of surgeries isn't yet complete, but she couldn't stick around for the next one. She had to flee. The word on the street was that Desastre wanted to kill her for having survived the attack and being able to land him back in prison. So her family had scrambled to cobble together money enough to send her to the States, desperate to save her life by having her disappear.

Her grandma had packed a backpack with snacks, jeans, and a jacket. Her mother couldn't stop sobbing and mourned in the corner. Her uncles worked on logistics. The whole thing was terrifying. Karla was confused. Her head throbbed relentlessly. She didn't want to go, but her family said she had to. She didn't understand how there was no alternative. She protested, saying she'd never leave Soyapango, let alone El Salvador. She said she knew neither the destination nor the route. She said she knew no English. All she knew was that she had to flee because her family said so, even if she had little money, even if she spoke no English, even if her head was pounding with pain and she still had a hole in her skull requiring follow-up surgery.

She leans towards me and drops her head, telling me to feel the open wound in her head. I decline, but she insists. I decline again, and she grabs two of my fingers. She guides them through her long hair to the soft and squishy wound. It's about the size of a quarter and feels raised, like a blister. Still looking down, she tells me *Tío* Elber helped her to the bus station, where she embarked in tears.

I withdraw my fingers and close my eyes, breathing deeply to try to keep my composure. It's something I've battled with before in here; this place is filled with horrible stories.

When Karla goes on to describe how she watched her *tío*, her town, her life in El Salvador disappear through the bus window, it takes all of my self-discipline to keep from weeping. And I want to hug her, but I don't dare; I'd risk expulsion from the detention center for the physical contact. So I draw back, unnaturally distancing myself from a hurt child in need of comfort and tenderness. I praise her for her strength, her courage, and her love for her family. I also tell her I'm so very sorry she's gone through all that, I'm so very sorry she's still in such terrible pain. I tell her I can try to help, if she'd like. I ask her, "What, if anything, can I do for you?"

Before she can answer, the demands of the workshop pull us apart, twigs scattered by a burst of wind. A guard at the front station is beckoning me to him, and a child named Raúl sees this and raises his hand, wanting to ask me something too. So I can't sit here any longer with Karla, as much as it pains me to leave her. But to stay here might mean more hurt. Were I to ignore the guard, then I could be reprimanded and thereby compromise my very permission to be here. I also owe Raúl some attention, as I do the rest of the children in here. After all, every child is in serious pain and need, however diverse their specifics. And that is not to diminish the urgent, excruciating agony of life for Karla, who is uniquely suffering and in need of medical attention.

Nevertheless, the reality is that I have to maintain good relations with staff in order to lead poetry workshops not only on this cellblock, but also on all the others too. And while not all of the refugee children in here have survived attempted rape, many write and discuss in workshop how they've been shot, beaten, stabbed, abused, neglected, and severely depressed.

So I zip over to the guard and answer his question, then hustle to Raúl. A stout Nicaraguan boy with a faint mustache, he's easygoing and smart, and I adore him. He has a cherubic face, a good sense of humor, and hands that dance like darting birds whenever he speaks. He's also one of those charming people who's quick to chuckle. He and I share a laugh together at some point during almost every workshop, but right now Raúl is serious. His eyes are narrowed to slits of concern. When I squat beside him for his question, he purses his lips for a silent moment, and then sputters words, struggling to articulate whatever it is that's bothering him.

After a series of starts and stops, he finally explains it: he wants to know why the "darker brother" of the poem has to sit in another room. He tells me it offends him, but he can't fully understand why. because he doesn't know why it was done in the first place. I thank him for the question, telling him it's at the heart of the poem and it's something we might discuss with the whole group. I ask him if that's ok, and when he consents, I rise at his side and interrupt the quiet industry of the room by posing Raúl's question loudly to everyone.

What ensues is a poignant discussion of discrimination across the hemispheric Americas. The children know all too well that racism exists, though some of its manifestations are new to them, like the US Jim Crow system. Hence Raúl's confusion, which it turns out was shared by most every child in the room. Once resolving it, they grasp the poem better and begin to respond to Hughes with examples of racism that they themselves have experienced. Some share how they've been insulted for the color of their skin, often by total strangers. Others speak of having been beaten for it by their hometown police. Still others tell of having been chased, robbed, and assaulted for it while migrating here. They also break my heart with their innocence. More than one child speaks of wanting asylum here because of a belief in the United States as a safe haven against racism.

Their conversation broadens further still, gaining steam, as they broach additional forms of discrimination they've endured: not only for the color of their skin, but also for being poor, Indigenous, orphaned, and tattooed. They scratch and claw to find the language to share their battered but intact pride in their roots, their identities, what they've withstood. It's a robust and ranging conversation, full of varied perspectives and insights, and I'm struck by the compassion of their thinking and the honesty of their introspection.

They do not hesitate to cite examples of their own ignorance in the past, talking through their mistakes and confessing to residual shame. In response, their peers are encouraging. They offer flashes of empathy, humor, and hope. It uplifts the speaker, as do subsequent comments about the various triumphs of those who've shared examples of terrible hardship and violence, and how they've overcome it and are still here.

Like this we chug along, lost in earnest conversation. As a professional educator, I cannot help but note their aptitude for careful listening. It is the engine that drives their ideas and binds them into this supportive group. The conversation is not easy, but it is existentially honest and welcoming to everyone. The children are patient and thoughtful. By listening empathetically, they are able to hear and acknowledge their differences with respect and curiosity. For these reasons and more, it strikes me that this cellblock of incarcerated teen boys and girls, many of whom struggle to read, counts among the best groups of students with whom I've worked over the past twenty years.

In other words, they're regular teenagers in that they thrive with adult guidance and encouragement. All they need to blossom is the opportunity. In the meantime, Karla has her head down, trying to wait out the pain.

CHAPTER 9

~~~~~

Digital Activism:
The Yang

While round us bark the mad and hungry dogs . . .

— CLAUDE McKAY

"We won't survive another day here," Wisien tells me, his voice a rushed, scared whisper.

We're on WhatsApp, speaking hurriedly, with much to say but our time is short, our connection fragile, the app glitchy.

I'm at home in Charlottesville, Virginia, while Wisien is in hiding in Piedras Negras, Coahuila. And however frantic he sounds, I'm thrilled to hear his voice.

He missed our scheduled call yesterday. I'd been worried sick ever since. It wasn't like him to go silent, and I understood all too well the danger he was in. We'd been talking daily for more than three weeks, often multiple times per day, and never before had he ghosted me. He knew the stakes were too high and our plan too intricate.

We were aiming for nothing less than for his three cousins and him to walk safely into the United States by permission of the US government. Perhaps even more ambitiously, we were attempting to coordinate all of this by cell phone, on

157

WhatsApp, with the men in hiding, trying to elude death threats.

It's one of the wonders of social media that an app could become a tool for guiding refugees to safety. In our case, we were using WhatsApp to swap not only texts, voicemails, and phone calls, but also documents, photos, encouraging memes, detailed maps, and logistics.

With each exchange, we were creating the pathway for Wisien and his cousins to walk safely to the border, cross a heavily militarized international bridge, meet a CBP contact, and seek asylum here by governmental invitation.

The plan derived from the brilliant minds of two US immigration attorneys, who were overseeing the project, which was still in its alpha phase. If/when proven successful, their blueprint would be shared across the country with other immigration groups seeking to help non-Mexican refugee families trapped in Mexico by MPP.

In the meantime, I was one of a handful of volunteers on the project. My role was to serve as a de facto case manager for each family that the two lead attorneys assigned me.

This meant I was their bilingual-Spanish point person, directing the international coordination of each family's safe crossing into the United States in collaboration with multiple agencies, agents, courts, and institutions on both sides of the border.

This began each time with me connecting with a family. Our first contact was most often by WhatsApp message. Together we would then arrange a good time for family members to talk by phone call or video chat. In that conversation, I would explain our project to them. If they liked our offer and decided to retain our services, which were completely free and comprehensive, then our collaboration would begin in earnest.

This often took multiple attempts across several days. A family had no reason to trust us initially, and they were subsisting in the shadows in Mexico under dire conditions. All family members were under threat of death, in hiding, and penniless in an unknown country where they had neither family nor friends. So they were scared, isolated, and hungry. This was true for all the families with which we worked.

Thanks to their courage, mutual trust would eventually be established, and I would begin to interview each family member to create their legal case. All the while, I was working with and for the family on multitude fronts on both sides of the border, bustling behind the scenes to try to keep them safe in Mexico while initiating petitions in federal US court and soliciting protections in Mexico too. Simultaneously, I was also remaining as available to the family as possible.

Needless to say, the work was challenging. In its most basic sense, my job involved me helping family members simply to endure. I marveled daily at their heroic fight to save and transform their lives.

Simultaneously, there was no small amount of pressure on me. In order for the family to succeed in safely entering the asylum process in the United States, I had to succeed as their chief advocate on both sides of the Mexico-US border. This often felt to me like I was walking a razor-thin high wire in strong wind and rain without a net beneath me. Because were I to fail, then the family would be denied entry to the United States, dashing their chance of getting asylum for at least ten years.

On top of that, all of the cases were difficult to manage because they were culturally complex and urgent. This resulted in me having to foster and maintain quick and sturdy alliances among our partners, who were sometimes political or ideological enemies.

Meanwhile, I was still traveling the world as poet, teaching full time at my university, parenting my two sons, supporting a depressed wife, helping to edit two literary magazines, writing academic texts, and coaching youth soccer, among many other duties, responsibilities, and pleasures.

Amidst all this scheduling, I prioritized serving the refugee families. I would go from a faculty meeting to my office on campus, where I would converse with an international matrix of demanding figures that included US federal judges, US Border Patrol agents, ICE agents, US immigration attorneys, Mexican clergy, Mexican shelter managers, Mexican activists, and many others. Typically, I only paused my coordination when a university student would stop by my office to ask a question about an upcoming essay or exam, or when a colleague would stop in with an academic concern.

Such was the context of Wisien's case. It involved a mosaic of people in Honduras, Mexico, and the United States, many of whom were reluctant but crucial partners in his hopes for asylum in the United States. Thankfully, my work had been going well, at least until Wisien disappeared on me yesterday.

It couldn't have happened at a worse time. We were just about set for his family and him to cross into the United States. We were simply waiting, or not so simply waiting, for the final major piece of the puzzle to fall into place: at any moment I'd receive a text message with the decision of a US federal judge on our petition for permission for Wisien and his family to enter the United States together as refugees seeking asylum.

Once having proof of that precious paperwork in hand, I would signal for Wisien and his cousins to dare to emerge from hiding in Piedras Negras and enact our plan for safe passage. We had already established the route, the contacts, and the means for them to inch their way from hiding to the International Bridge leading into Eagle Pass, Texas. It was a perilous part of the journey, requiring the family to avoid cartels, gangs, corrupt Mexican officials, and other potentially devastating interlopers. If the family were to make it successfully to the Eagle Pass Port of Entry, run by US CBP, then they would be received there by a waiting and ready Border Patrol agent, as I had prearranged for them all through a CBP contact.

Now here is the possibly confusing part: if all went well at the Eagle Pass Point of Entry with CBP, then the attending Border Patrol agent would detain Wisien and his cousins.

That was our plan—detention—however counterintuitive and frightening as it may seem. We *wanted* the family to be detained because the alternative was for them to be expelled immediately from the country by MPP. But once detained in the United States, the family could file their claims for asylum as refugees. That is also to say that every step of the family's journey, including detention, was purposefully and meticulously designed by the two brilliant attorneys leading our project. And I stood behind them like the rest of our volunteer team, ready and able to dutifully enact the process through any lawful means available to us.

To that end, before Wisien had disappeared, I'd been working on securing a member of the Mexican clergy in Piedras Negras to escort the family on foot to the International Bridge. This practice had been developed as a means to help our clients to avoid potential problems with not only the aforementioned criminals, gangsters, city police, politicos, and federal agents in Mexico at and around the border, but also refugee-hating locals. All posed a risk of waylaying if not undermining the refugees' journey from hiding to detention.

However, if all went as planned, then the clergyperson would bid farewell to Wisien and his cousins at the start of the bridge. They would then begin the final leg of their Mexican trek by walking as a physically unaccompanied foursome across the border.

Even here, though, they would be actively supported by my project. Wisien would have one of the project's pro bono immigration attorneys on active standby on his cellphone, set to intervene and help however necessary. This, too, was tightly coordinated. The attorney would be punctual, available, and up to date on Wisien's case via my updates. The attorney also would wait poised without distraction to take action to defend the family by any means available to them, if necessary.

Thankfully, such action was rarely needed by our clients because, as aforementioned, we would only send them across the bridge to the international border and into the custody of a Border Patrol agent after having already received permission from a federal judge in the United States for them to enter the country.

And by the grace of the gods, all of this intricate planning had been coming together fantastically for Wisien and his family. The time to cross the bridge was mere days away. Then Wisien vanished.

He left me no trace. No text message. No indication of an attempted call. No voicemail. No photo. In response to my worried flurry of texts after he missed our meeting, he didn't even send me an emoji in reply, not even one smiley face, which was his favorite.

And as much as I'd tried not to worry about him or his cousins, I did. It was only natural. I'd grown close to the family, as most often happens with my clients in these cases. And how wouldn't I? Our work together was intimate, intensive, and sustained, typically spanning many weeks. Through it, I'd come to know these people well, learning their struggles, hopes, fears, and dreams.

In this manner I would come to admire each person in the project and root for them wholeheartedly. I was deeply invested emotionally in their well-being in hiding and in life moving forward in perpetuity.

I think that most people would respond similarly. To build a family's case for court, for example, they had to explain to me in explicit detail the exact violence that had forced them to flee their country of origin, as well as their subsequent and frequent suffering while migrating to the Mexico-US border.

I felt honored by their trust. They would regularly recount to me personal histories involving assaults, kidnappings, robberies, rapes, torture, murders, and death threats. This only intensified my commitment to serve them. And this is precisely how and why I was doggedly working for Wisien's family, which I liked and admired a great deal. Then he disappeared.

I had come to know Wisien as a sweet, bright, and gentle nineteen-year-old man full of love and creativity. I knew he aspired to become a US citizen, work in hospitality, adopt a dog from a shelter, go to college, and discover a career. Despite his fear in hiding, he regularly sent me warm, personal words of thanks and of encouragement for me in my work for his family. He sent me positive memes and emojis, as well as photos of the family in happier times and whilst migrating.

His three cousins, who are biological brothers, were equally amicable, idealistic, and earnest. They ranged in age from eighteen to twenty-three and had diverse dreams for their lives in the States as students and professionals.

Together, the four men formed a phenomenally close and supportive family unit. Like the kindest of families, they shared a deep and nourishing tenderness and commitment. This bonded them strongly into the mutually supportive unit that had kept them alive through their harrowing history.

They hailed from a tight-knit Garifuna community in a rough neighborhood in San Pedro Sula, Honduras. They had grown up together like four loving brothers, not three brothers and one cousin. Long before their forced migration, their bond had helped them to weather many years of withering discrimination. As aforementioned, they were Garifuna, meaning here that they'd endured a steady slew of anti-Black and anti-Indigenous bigotry in school, at work, and in the street.

Additionally, they'd been dealing with the ugly scourge of homophobia for the past four years. It all began when Wisien came out as gay to the local community. This drew the immediate ire of certain family members, friends, and neighbors. Somehow those people felt betrayed by Wisien and began to mistreat him. Even his own mother abused him, eventually throwing him out of their apartment and disowning him. It was then that he'd found refuge in the special shelter of his cousins' love and home.

More specifically, he moved into their small, rented one-bedroom apartment. There they lived in harmony and health, happy amongst themselves. But that peace was shattered when they began to receive death threats, forcing them to flee.

In retrospect, the turning point was probably not those death threats, but rather Hurricane Eta. Despite the poverty and violence in their neighborhood, the family of four had been doing relatively well in their apartment until the hurricane hit.

It ravaged and flooded their neighborhood, ruining homes, clinics, schools, and markets. It also closed the restaurant in which one of Wisien's cousins worked washing dishes. And it wiped out the construction job that another of the cousins had just lucked into.

On top of that the men's landlord tried to raise their rent. It was a desperate, despicable move. Money was tight for him, as it was for almost everyone, so he'd thought to squeeze his tenants for a few extra lempiras.

But Wisien and his cousins protested. They said that in the wake of the hurricane, they could no longer make their original rent, let alone pay it with an increase.

The landlord demurred, demanding angrily that they pay the new rent or be evicted.

In their final confrontation, Wisien's oldest cousin, Iwani, slammed the door in the landlord's face. Infuriated, he responded by loosing a vicious string of threats and anti-Black curses at the family.

Among other things, he warned them that his son was the leader of the local gang. Wisien and his cousins ignored the claim. They'd never before seen the landlord with any family, let alone a son, so they thought him bluffing in a fit of rage.

But later that same night, bluster turned to truth. A car pulled up outside the apartment and five tattooed men piled out. They headed directly to the family's home, where one of the gangsters banged loudly on the front door.

He called out to Iwani by name.

At Iwani's instruction, the family stayed crouched and silent inside their home with the lights off, Wisien once recounted, trembling with fear. He knew all too well what local gangs could do, including recent murders by machete and by machine gun.

The man at the door began to shout through it, saying that the landlord was his father and that the family had better pay the new rent in full by noon tomorrow. If not, they'd be killed. No excuses.

Wisien and his cousins were scared witless. They didn't have the money, even if they'd wanted to pay. They quickly gathered what they could carry in backpacks, and before sunrise they'd fled Honduras for good.

Their ensuing plan, made in panicked haste, was as rudimentary as it was spontaneous: head for the United States to begin life anew there, together, in safety.

Setting off, they tried to draw strength from their hopeful dispositions. They spoke of finding good jobs in construction, restaurants, and hotels, like former acquaintances who'd migrated in the past and sent back word of their experiences. And Wisien, who loved US TV and movies, talked dreamily about still other possibilities, like finding work in sun-splashed country clubs and ritzy marinas.

But there would be nothing glamorous or ritzy about their forced migration. It would prove a relentlessly brutal journey from the beginning.

As aforementioned, the family was Garifuna, meaning they were both Black and Indigenous, and they spoke Garifuna among themselves, proud of their heritage. Plus, Wisien was openly gay. And, sadly, all of those wonderful aspects of their identities made the men conspicuous targets for bigots and criminals throughout their journey.

Consequently, long before even reaching any border town along the Mexico-US border and being forced into hiding there by the most recent death threats, the four men had already been repeatedly assaulted, robbed, abused, and threatened with death by a multitude of hateful people.

For example, just after crossing the border from Honduras into Guatemala, the family was robbed of their last lempiras. They'd been searching for a bus station to try to head to Mexico when a group of young men jumped and robbed them.

Within a week of that attack, the family was again beaten in the street, this time in central Mexico. There three young men had begun the fracas verbally, hurling anti-Black and anti-immigrant insults at the family. That escalated to a physical beating in broad daylight. Of the assault, Wisien recounted curling up into a ball on the sidewalk, closing his eyes, and covering his head while strikes and insults rained down all over him.

Soon after, in yet another Mexican town, they were robbed of their remaining belongings except for the clothes on their backs. That indignity concluded with the family being chased off by the assailants yelling threats and slurs at them for being Black.

Somewhat similarly, they'd been kicked out of a line for a free meal from a Mexican church for their skin color, and they'd been run out of a camp for migrating people for the same reason, being told they were too dark to sleep there.

Such bigoted violence followed the family all the way into Piedras Negras, where they'd planned to cross the border as soon as possible, for safety. But that plan was sundered soon after their arrival by a combination of MPP and local violence.

More specifically, on their second day in town, while still learning from other refugees about MPP and the options for crossing the border, the family was forced to scramble into hiding by death threats from a local gang or cartel. They couldn't say which.

It all began innocently enough. Wisien had entered a bodega around midday to buy a jug of distilled water for the family. But another shopper soon started to pick on Wisien, hissing homophobic slurs at him while he was in line for the register.

It's hard to know exactly why Wisien had attracted the man's ire and hate. Regardless, the homophobic slurs soon swerved into anti-Black and anti-migrant insults too.

Perhaps MPP played a role in it. Tensions had been running high in Piedras Negras, as in many border towns, due to the influx of migrating people and refugees. Locals were irritated by the ballooning numbers of trapped and impoverished people. Xenophobia was surging.

This bigot in the bodega was clearly one such angry xenophobe. His aspersions included the claim that migrating people were trashing his neighborhood, his city. He said they were crude and dirty. He told Wisien to scram and never reappear.

Ever a sweet, gentle, and nonconfrontational person, Wisien tried to de-escalate the situation by simply abandoning the jug of water and leaving the bodega. But the man followed, continuing to curse Wisien in the street.

Soon a group of local men materialized, encircling Wisien and his cousins, who had been waiting for him. They were about to be beaten yet again.

Just then a truck pulled up. Armed men in plain clothes poured out. They took over the situation in a way that made Wisien think, at first, they were police.

They brusquely quieted the locals, who obeyed. And then they barked an ultimatum at Wisien and his cousins: "Give us your money and leave Piedras Negras—or we'll kill you."

Wisien and his cousins took the threat seriously. They'd been warned in the refugee camp to avoid the local gangs and cartels at all costs. They quickly handed over the few Mexican pesos they'd accumulated and took off running, feeling both terrified of being shot in the back and grateful for being allowed the chance to flee.

In a panicked blur, Wisien and his cousins ran for their lives through unknown streets in a foreign city. They were scared, and soon they were lost on the outskirts of Piedras Negras.

The sun was setting and they were exhausted when they came across an abandoned ranch. They'd been robbed penniless, and they were crashing after the burst of adrenaline from the confrontation.

As a short-term fix, they decided it best to try to hide on the ranch for the night. As far as they could discern, it was deserted, and they could therefore use it as a safe place to rest up, at least for the night.

It was from that ranch the next day that Wisien and I had first connected. He'd reached out to my project from the refugee camp in Piedras Negras, where he'd heard good things about our work. His request had made itself to my directors, who assigned his case to me, so there he and I were, conversing over WhatsApp.

It turned out to be a terrific stroke of luck that the men had stumbled across the abandoned ranch. One night of emergency shelter bloomed into three weeks of sanctuary. Sure, they struggled to find enough food and drink nearby, but the family felt safe whenever on the property, including at night.

And each day, Wisien and I spoke, advancing the plan. Our collaboration was all the easier because our personalities had synced from the start. He was sweet, open, and smart, even when our conversations were thick with painful truths.

For instance, from our very first call, I explained to him how honored I was by the chance to try to help his family, but that our plan was a longshot at best.

I went on to detail both how and why the United States had essentially closed the border to non-Mexican refugees like him with tactics like MPP. I also added that even if his family were lucky enough to make it across the border and request asylum in the States, they would only be just *beginning* an immigration process that would take roughly two years to wend its way to completion through the US immigration system. Moreover, I made it clear to him, as I'd been trained to do, that the two-year pursuit of asylum from within the

United States would cost his family a great deal financially and emotionally, and that only after that entire, lengthy process would the fate of his family finally be decided. The courts would only then finally declare whether the family could stay in the States as asylees or whether they'd be deported and barred from reentering the United States for a minimum of ten years.

Of course, I'd also explained to Wisien from the start, too, that our plan had strong legal merit. I shared with him that my project had in fact already been very successful in multiple US courts for multiple families through this very plan and that I was hoping for the same result in his case. Plus, as I lamented openly to him, this plan was really the only option right now for non-Mexican people wanting to cross the border and seek asylum.

I remember Wisien asking me politely at that point to please pause for a moment.

I could hear him turn away from his phone and have a brief discussion in Garifuna with his family.

Returning to me, he then said with succinct confidence that his family was in. He said their goal was asylum, they wanted to try my plan, and they would follow my lead.

Wisien quickly proved a joy to work for, even on uncomfortable aspects of the plan, like discussions of the experiences driving his fear of living in Honduras and Mexico. Even when afraid and fatigued, he remained hopeful. Maybe it was the optimism of youth. Maybe it was his warm and gentle spirit.

Regardless, I hustled to build his case, working on it seven days per week and at all hours. I was doing everything I could for the family, as I did for every client, knowing they lived in imminent danger. In other words, my empathy for each family fueled my work ethic, and I worked at a sprinter's pace for them. Concurrently, I knew equally well that my frenzied pace was unsustainable.

I knew I was already long burned out. My psychologist and I discussed it in almost every session each week. Simply put, I was juggling far too many responsibilities and projects in my immigration work alone, not to mention my many other responsibilities and duties as husband, father, teacher, poet, literary translator, scholar, and guest speaker traveling around the world by invitation. Plus, I was recovering poorly from a hip replacement surgery, which further battered my spirit. In short, I was exhausted physically and emotionally, and I was in constant pain, leading to me being depressed and friable. Still, onward I pushed. I had to. However depleted I felt, this was a special project. I couldn't resist participating in it. It was filled with hope.

Hope was an exceedingly rare and precious jewel in immigration work, and I had lucked into a project that was flush with it. Best of all, the hope wasn't illusory; it was real. I could even enumerate it: I had won every single case I'd put forth for clients with this project, as had my colleagues with their clients. It was incredible. Dozens of refugee families had escaped extraordinary violence and poverty and were living safely in the United States, pursuing asylum here.

That kind of direct, immediate impact was as personally gratifying as the project's overall success was statistically idiosyncratic. It was so rare in fact as to be unprecedented. Such triumph was wildly unheard of, and wildly heartening, in immigration circles.

Even speaking anecdotally, in all of my years of experience in the fields of immigration reform and justice, I would guesstimate that the most successful projects on which I'd worked had won around 10 percent of our cases in court. And most of our projects likely tallied a winning percentage in the low single digits.

But not with this project. We were unfailingly helping people to reach safety and start asylum proceedings in the United States, even with the border being officially closed.

Here, it bears mention, too, that I was relatively untrained and unprepared for such sensitive and crucial work. Sure, I studied it and attended pertinent conferences, but always as a literary scholar and poet first and foremost. And I am neither a paralegal nor attorney nor psychiatrist nor psychologist. But as ill-suited as I may have been for the role, I played it because I had to. I had the opportunity to join the project and help human beings in need.

More specifically, I possessed the linguistic, interpersonal, and cultural skills to fulfill the task of compiling the content needed for legal arguments for each case, as evident in the incontrovertible truth that my team was winning in court and my clients were realizing their wishes to pursue asylum in the States.

Still, we might pause to wonder how good an immigration system is when it has poets working with traumatized refugees in hiding in another country as their therapist, legal counsel, and social worker, instead of people with actual expertise in those highly learned, crucial fields?

Thankfully, despite my inadequacies, Wisien and his cousins had almost made it successfully into the United States, as was their greatest goal. After weeks of brutal agony and deprivation on the road to the border, they were on the cusp of crossing it. Then Wisien disappeared on me.

His disappearance surprised me like a hard slap to my cheek from a quiet, gentle friend.

I had known Wisien was anxious about the protocol for crossing the international bridge, and especially the idea of

turning himself in on purpose to armed and uniformed offi-
cials, but I had not imagined that he could be rattled enough
to quit on the plan. But with our missed meeting, that was
among my first concerns.

I had been assuring him that his cousins and he *wanted*
to be detained, even though, as I'd repeatedly explained to
him, as to every client, that this included the very real risk of
a prolonged detention in an immigration detention center,
and possibly even family separation. Nevertheless, it was their
best option.

Even reading that proposal now to myself, I can hear how
it might sound farfetched to a client, if not downright insane.
Everything they'd done was to remain safe by avoiding capture
while migrating. And every single refugee family with whom
I'd worked on this project had spoken to me of having been
traumatized in the past by armed and uniformed officers, with
the violence ranging from extortion to robbery to assault to
rape.

And now, after I'd implored them for weeks to stay safe
by remaining carefully hidden from any armed and uniformed
official, I was asking them to leave the relative safety of their
hiding places and walk openly through town, hopefully
avoiding cartel and gang members, and into the arms of an
armed and uniformed US border agent, to turn themselves in?

Moreover, I was suggesting that they not only wanted to
be detained, but that they would be risking prolonged deten-
tion, and possibly family separation. But that was the plan, as
designed by two highly respected, experienced, and compas-
sionate US immigration attorneys, and it was working.

I worried, too, that Wisien had missed our meeting against
his will. Besides Mexican officials, cartel and gang members
regularly patrolled the town to extort migrating people. So I

was certainly concerned for Wisien's immediate physical safety and that of his cousins.

To channel my worry into something productive, I set to work on stabilizing Wisien's case while I waited to hear from him. I'd come to understand exactly how and why his family and he so desperately needed asylum. I knew the violence that had scarred them and the wounds that were still bleeding. And I reached out to our connections on both sides of the border to fortify the infrastructure for a crossing that I was hoping to set in motion at any moment.

For strength, I also looked at photos and messages from prior clients, now in the States pursuing asylum claims. Prior to being assigned Wisien's case, every single refugee family with whom I'd worked on this project had included young children. And their innocence in all of this, and their extreme suffering as children in it, added not only extra weight to the heavy load of responsibility buckling my shoulders, but also encouragement in so far as their lives were now safer and filled with real hope.

The truth is, though, that no single person or group could deliver the justice needed by refugees. What *is* needed is large-scale reform to governmental policy and legislation and a reformulation of our thinking about migrating people and refugees. Because if we as human beings are capable of recognizing and helping those in need among us—and I believe we are—then that help should be given to the best of our ability.

In the absence of such reform, refugees will continue to suffer like Wisien and his family on their respective journeys. Their experiences will continue to be unduly and unnecessarily stressful, dangerous, and injurious. We who try to help them, too, will continue to be able to offer few solutions—which brings me back to Wisien.

My phone rang.

"I'm sorry I missed you yesterday," Wisien is saying, his tone sadder and more despairing than I've ever heard It. "It's been really difficult. I don't know if we'll make it."

He goes on to summarize for me what his cousins and he have been going through in the past twenty-four hours.

Sadly, it's a story I've heard many times before from refugees, however much the details may vary by the person. What remains consistent across the stories are the major qualifiers of hunger, exposure, exhaustion, despair, fear, and violence.

In Wisien's case, it all began yesterday morning, when an unknown truck rolled into the ranch, parking at the front door. A *narcocorrido* was blaring from its radio, and as is well known, this was cartel country.

"Thankfully," Wisien explains, "the music arrived on the wind before the truck itself appeared."

That musical prelude gave Wisien and his cousins just enough time to scramble into the hills behind the ranch to hide. From there, crouched behind boulders and desert shrubs, they watched six men exit the truck and enter the home.

It was a windy winter morning, and as Wisien and his cousins watched in t-shirts, having fled without even their jackets, they shivered not only with the icy cold, but also fear. They dared not move a muscle to warm their bodies, or even whisper to one another about what they were seeing. They knew the violence of the cartels. So there they stayed, freezing in the hills, hungry, anxious, and praying for the men to leave.

Morning became afternoon became frosty evening. Still the truck hadn't moved. Still Wisien and his cousins remained hidden.

They didn't know what else to do but stay put. At some point they fell mercifully to sleep, huddled in a heap for warmth like a litter of puppies.

When they woke at dawn, a pale sun shone on the horizon. It was freezing out, and they were hungry. The truck was gone, but they had no idea if any of the men had stayed behind in the house below.

So they remained hidden, watching and waiting all morning. By noon, they hadn't seen any movement in the house, nor had the truck returned.

Iwani, their de facto leader, brokered a tense family discussion in quick, hissed whispers. Ultimately, they voted to abandon the home and head for the town center on foot via the hills. They knew the route would be more physically rigorous than walking the streets, but they'd be safe from passing vehicles.

They were certainly tired, cold, and weak from hunger, thirst, and rough sleep, but at least they would stay relatively hidden in the rugged landscape by choosing the more arduous route. So off they went, single file, bent low, following Iwani through the hills. Like this they walked a winding path over rugged terrain, their mouths as dry as sand, their bellies howling for food.

Wisien recalls feeling lightheaded and weak as he trudged on, trying to concentrate on following one heavy foot with the other.

After about forty-five minutes of inching through the hills, their legs and arms burning and scratched by brush, they came at last upon a building: a modest church on the town's outskirts.

During their migration from Honduras to Mexico, churches hadn't always proven welcoming to them, but they were too exhausted now to worry. They swung open the front door and piled in, ready to beg anyone present for mercy, water, food.

But the sanctuary was empty. They collectively exhaled both disappointment and relief: at least they wouldn't be shooed back into the desert midwinter. Iwani laid himself down gently on a pew on his belly to rest. He was soon asleep.

Wisien searched the nave for an electrical outlet to charge his dead cell phone and found one in a back corner. He knew WhatsApp was their life buoy in a torrential storm at sea; the app could pull them through crashing waves to a better future. Once regaining enough battery to light up his screen, Wisien saw my stockpile of text messages. He immediately replied that yes, his cousins and he were ok but needed to talk as soon as possible.

"We're cold, tired, and afraid," he writes. "I don't think we can wait another day. We have no food or money, and we lost our place to sleep and wait."

I grimace because the date of their crossing is still at least two days away. We not only need the court's decision before being ready to contact the Border Patrol agents at the Eagle Pass Port of Entry, but also a CBP agent there to confirm with me their willingness, date, and time to receive at their convenience the four refugees.

That's when my phone rang.

"What should we do?" Wisien asks softly, almost to the heavens instead of me.

As I pause to think, I can hear his fear in his quickened breathing. It's yet another sad detail that I've come to recognize in this work. I've heard it too many times before, from too many previous clients, on too many terrified phone calls after mishaps, with human beings crouched in hiding to escape death and find a way to reach safety and freedom. It is also the fear in feeling trapped in place without any idea if the future even exists.

I cannot overstate how excruciating the waiting is for clients. In this instance, it was pushing Wisien and his family to teeter on the brink of a mental health disaster. They were as close to their breaking point as to their border-crossing. Would the family members make it through these final grueling days and become asylees in the States, or would they snap under the intense pressure and make an impulsive decision with devastating, lifelong consequences?

"I'll call you in two hours," I tell him, and we hang up.

It might sound cold, but his best chance lies in working the plan instead of commiserating with me by phone. And I had work to do for the family, work I couldn't do while talking with him.

From my office in Virginia, I set to work activating a transnational network of support for Wisien and his cousins, both within and beyond this project. It was a whirlwind of activity because I had to teach in fifteen minutes.

In a flurry of emails and texts, I reach out to people across the United States and Mexico. Each works for immigration reform in their own capacity, and their knowledge is as vast and varied as their hearts are open and huge.

I am talking about lawyers, professors, physicians, therapists, social workers, community organizers, journalists, artists, retirees, university students, librarians, pastors, rabbis, priests, chefs, school principals, and more. And through their ongoing work for migrating people and refugees, they have cohered into a compassionate and responsive supplement to the official immigration system spanning Mexico and the United States. And to this day, my admiration runs deep for each and every one of these people from whom I draw much strength and inspiration. In my mind, they are a glittering constellation of the finest kinds of people you could hope to meet in life. They have committed their days to diminishing the suffering of others and to creating more harmonious, healthy, and inclusive communities.

With that network engaged and updated on the urgency of Wisien's case, I rush off to teach my class. Once it ends, I jump into my email and find a bunch of helpful answers from those amazing immigration advocacy people. And I'm soon on WhatsApp with Wisien, relaying to him his options for how his cousins and he might choose to stay safe in Piedras Negras until the date of their crossing, which I reiterate should occur within three days max.

They have a quick family discussion and then Wisien tells me his family and he would like to try to reach safer shelter. He says that however dangerous the walk from the church, they need to try to find somewhere safe to sleep and, ideally, something to eat. Before hanging up, we agree to talk again in the early evening.

Hours later, as I'm commuting home, I receive word that the courts have approved the family's petition to cross at Eagle Pass. I pull off the highway, text Wisien the great news, and then query the preferences of the CBP agents at the Eagle Pass Port of Entry for the time and day of that crossing.

Two days later, at 7 a.m., as requested by a CBP agent, Wisien and his cousins walk across the bridge without incident and present themselves for detention.

Despite knowing they risk prolonged detention, and even family separation, they greet the agent and enter the station with their heads held high, having made it this far.

Thankfully, all goes smoothly at the station, with the agent recognizing their legal petition as well as the men's credible fear of returning both to Mexico and to Honduras.

He begins their paperwork for a family-based asylum claim predicated upon their protected status, meaning they've suffered persecution for their race, religion, nationality, membership in a particular social group, and/or political opinions.

At 5:36 p.m. that afternoon, Wisien next reaches out to me through WhatsApp from a street corner in Eagle Pass, Texas. He's gushing words of gratitude between tears of relief, happiness, and hope. He thanks his God, and he thanks the United States, and he thanks the Border Patrol agent at the station for processing his family and keeping them together. He thanks my group and me, and most importantly, he declares euphorically that, at last, he is safe, he is here.

CHAPTER 10

Harvested Fruit

*We are all bound up together in one great
bundle of humanity.*

— FRANCES ELLEN WATKINS HARPER

P resident Trump's family separation policy, called "Zero Tolerance," pulled more than 5,000 children from the arms of their parents.[1]

In response, public outrage in the United States was loud, emphatic, and widespread.[2] The vast majority of the nation was incredulous to the president's willful cruelty, which contradicted both their values and the law.[3] It also contradicted our best medical understanding of children's health and well-being. The American Academy of Pediatrics, for example, explained that family separation causes "irreparable harm" to children.[4] The nonprofit group Physicians for Human Rights even classified family separation as "torture,"[5] echoing with medical expertise what legal experts had argued for years on the subject.[6] In fact, so many people from so many different sectors of the nation were so swift and adamant with their condemnation of the president's Zero Tolerance policy that he was only able to run his program officially from April of 2018 to November of 2018.

That termination of the policy in November of 2018 seemed a rare triumph of the ethics and goodwill of the American people over one of its more unethical and malicious politicians. We now know, though, that no such triumph existed: family separation occurred during the first Trump presidency for far longer than that seven-month window. His administration had in fact begun separating families at the Mexico-US border long before he officially launched the practice in April of 2018. We can trace it back almost to the beginning of his presidency, with records showing its inception in February of 2017, within a month of his taking office.[7] According to the US Congress and to the Trump administration itself, CBP had taken at least 856 children from their parents before the launch of Zero Tolerance.[8] Perhaps more chilling still, more than one-quarter of those children were younger than five years old.[9]

Those early figures would prove conservative.[10] Again, the government itself later acknowledged that it may have separated as many as 2,500 children from their parents before the official launch of Zero Tolerance.[11] However, such numbers are difficult to confirm with precision because the processes of family separation were so chaotic, haphazard, varied, and obscured. Further, these processes often involved multiple governmental agencies, transfers, and contradictory press conferences and statements by governmental officials.[12]

The resulting records are therefore diffuse and partial.[13] Even that lack of clear recordkeeping is frightening. If we truly cared about these children as human beings and respected their dignity, not to mention the humanity and dignity of their parents, then we would not take them from their parents in the first place. And if we did take them into federal custody, then we would at least keep track of them, and with great care.

Sadly, though, we did not and have not. In a report from the inspector general of Health and Human Services, it was found that the government lost track of at least 1,500 children in detention within a month of launching Zero Tolerance.[14] Worse still, it would be months, if not years, before most of those children would be reunited with their parents. In fact, as of late 2023, about 1,000 of the children had still not been located and reconnected with their parents by the Biden administration.[15] And that is despite the best efforts of the Family Reunification Task Force, which President Biden had created in 2021 expressly to reunite such families.

Additionally, according to a report from the Southern Poverty Law Center, the government serially violated court orders demanding an immediate stop to family separation. This occurred before, during, and after Zero Tolerance. Here again, reports are incomplete, scattered, and buried. Nevertheless, they combine to reveal a willful disregard for both federal law and public will. For example, in May of 2019, the Trump administration publicly attested to having separated at least 389 families *after* having knowingly received injunctions from the courts to cease and desist any such processes.[16]

One month later, in June of 2019, a group of journalists in an immigration detention center in Texas reported counting roughly 250 children who had been separated from their parents.[17] Those children ranged in age from infants to teens, and they had been held in that facility for at least twenty-seven days. This means that their detention violated federal law, including the federal Flores Settlement Agreement, which limits the detention of unaccompanied minors to a maximum of twenty days, and only with a special extension to reach that twenty-day limit. In this unlawful instance in June of 2019, the situation had turned so dire for the isolated children that the older ones had taken to caring for the younger ones, often despite being of no familial relation. Moreover, the journalists decried the conditions of the children's captivity as overcrowded, unhygienic, and lacking in food and water. And these were observations made by journalists visiting but one of our more than 270 immigration detention centers in the United States.[18]

Were that not troubling enough, there is also a long and sordid history of child abuse within immigrant detention centers. This has been repeatedly reported by such credible sources as *The New York Times*, AP News, and National Public Radio (NPR).[19] Those reports detail, for example, that between October 2014 and July 2018, meaning the period overlapping my poetry workshops in the juvenile immigration detention center, there were more than 4,500 complaints of the sexual abuse of incarcerated undocumented children.[20] This adds an especially terrifying concern to any debate addressing the enduring use of family separation.

How, then, might we reconfigure our immigration infrastructure to ensure the safety and dignity of migrating people and refugees? And how might we better meet the needs of migrating families? We certainly have the expertise and resources to support them, as well as an awareness of the acute suffering of family members in separation, and especially children. What remains is to develop and fund the new framework for that improved immigration system, which would include not only a more humane engagement by the state of migrating people and refugees, but also a national cultivation in the public of their ability to see migrating people and refugees as human beings, deserving dignified treatment and lives.

A potential cornerstone of such a remastered framework could involve humane alternatives to detention (ATDs). Scholars, lawyers, social engineers, think tanks, social workers, healthcare workers, and many others have long been working on such ATDs in the United States and around the world, in such diverse places as Italy, Japan, Mexico, Spain, and

Tunisia.[21] Moreover, they have consistently proven successful when thoughtfully designed and implemented.

In the United States, for example, the Obama administration piloted a small but successful program introducing community-based ATDs in 2016, including healthcare, housing security, and job training. This kept families from being separated, cost less than detention, and had a superb compliance rate. According to reports by the Women's Refugee Commission, American Immigration Council, and by *Mother Jones*, 99 percent of participants made their every ICE check-in, and 100 percent made their court appearances.[22] Unfortunately, President Trump, upon taking office, abruptly canceled that promising pilot program rather than continue and develop it.

Nevertheless, we might resuscitate and build upon such precedents. These might include some kind of systematized combination of federal and community-based elements, such as residency permits, work visas, case management, healthcare, legal aid, childcare, and housing support, for example. That is but a quick sampling of previously successful elements of ATDs from around the country and world. The true limitations of such reform are the limitations of our imagination and our will.

Meanwhile, instead of innovating an immigration system that could prioritize the use of ATDs to help migrating people and refugees, who in turn would help the nation, we continue to fund and maintain a failing system. We continue to intentionally and knowingly hurt people each day, including many children.

Perhaps more problematically still, their suffering has been commodified within the US political economy. It is as lucrative as it is dehumanizing, and it has been integrated into the very foundation of the US economy. Our indifference to this truth allows for the smooth and steady perpetuation of our unjust, malevolent system. Children are turned into profit. Their very bodies become living commodities.[23]

The children in our poetry workshops understand this all too well. They recognize how their lives are transacted as commodities in privatized isolation cells. Facilities receive federal contracts to join the national network of immigration detention centers, and they are paid a daily rate for each occupied cell, as is customary in most federal contracts with private and semi-private immigration detention centers. This is a systemic disincentive to free children from detention as quickly as possible. Consequently, their suffering is protracted, and they understand its purpose in the US economy.

In workshop one morning, we were discussing precisely this. The children had been frustrated over the past weeks by word from the grapevine of dehumanizing rhetoric from the Trump administration about migrating people from Latin America working in agricultural jobs to jumpstart their new lives here. Understandably roiled,[24] the children had begun to write and converse regularly about their pride in their cultures of origin. From our conversation that morning, Gabriel wrote the following poem, *"De la tierra"* ["From the Earth"].

De la tierra
De la tierra creció una fruta,
Tan rica,
Que me puse a pensar,
¿Quién cosechó esa fruta?

From the Earth
From the earth grew a fruit
so delicious
I paused to wonder,
Who harvested this fruit?

When Gabriel, a boy with big dreams for his future as an attorney or teacher in the United States, first read aloud this poem to the workshop that morning, we sat in a brief harmony of stunned silence.

I remember thinking in awe, "How could such a young child—barely thirteen!—who was quintessentially sheepish, offer such a powerful punch in a mere four lines of poetry?"

The silence was finally broken not by a child but by Emelia, an official from the Office of Refugee Resettlement. She had asked to sit in on the workshops that morning, and I had agreed, but only after having polled the children for permission first, which they warmly granted unanimously.

"*¡Bravo!*" Emelia exclaimed after hearing the poem.

I remember Gabriel beaming with pride at her compliment. His peers then jumped in, calling out their own words of gratitude and praise for the poem.

"*Está bueno,*" nodded Jesús, his brow furrowed with affirmation.

"*Bien hecho,*" chimed in Ramón.

"*¡Excelente!*" said Estefania, smiling.

And soon we were discussing the agrarian labor market in the United States in general, and its experience from the perspective of undocumented people in particular. It was a broad and ranging conversation, with Emelia, too, participating. And were it not for the brutal conditions of detention and deprivation circumscribing us, then our conversation would appear to you no different than any of those lively and intelligent discussions that spring from my poetry workshops in universities, high schools, middle schools, literary festivals, arts centers, public libraries, and community centers.

I also share "*De la tierra*" here for another reason: I wish to acknowledge and celebrate not only Gabriel's brilliance, but also the brilliance of all of the poets in our workshops in the immigration detention center, not to mention the general brilliance of children as poets, regardless of time or place. Children are rich with imagination, much as they are rich with curiosity, vitality, and flexibility. It is one of the primary reasons why I have so enjoyed running workshops with young writers for nearly thirty years with great pleasure and admiration.

From such experience, and from extensive research for master's degrees and a Ph.D., I have come to understand how children flourish when feeling safe, loved, and supported by adults, who can guide their development, as teachers do throughout our schools across the nation and world. More darkly, then, Gabriel's poem exemplifies the brilliant minds of the thousands of children being denied a safe, sustained, and nourishing classroom experience in freedom by the US immigration system. Rather than encouraging their intrinsic brilliance to shine, we are dimming it with child detention, which deforms the children's minds, bodies, and lives.

On a different muggy, summer morning, the children were talking in workshop about precisely this dilemma of entrapment and deformation. The subject erupted from months of writing and talking with a deep, twisting pain in their guts from missing family, friends, girlfriends, and their own children. To try to help them to cope with their pain and grief, I had designed a workshop aiming to create the conditions for them to summon and share those thoughts and feelings in focused writing. Specifically, I thematized their past discussions into a notion of longing for frustrated love, and I structured it through research on expressive writing and trauma.

On this morning, this meant bringing in examples of poetry from writers with overlapping concerns and experiences to those of the children. I had therefore selected poems by José Antonio Burciaga from *Undocumented Love/Amor indocumentado*, poems from prison by Miguel Hernández, and poems from a cloistered Sor Juana Inés de la Cruz. As the children and I read, talked, and wrote about those poems, we munched on brightly colored sour gummy worms, a favorite of theirs.

From that supportive, freeing atmosphere, the children felt empowered to use poetry to brainstorm and debate strategies for keeping love alive in their hearts while being forced to live in excruciating pain in here. One of the most poignant poems to emerge from this is titled "*Si el hombre pudiera . . .*" ["If a man could . . ."].

Si el hombre pudiera . . .
llorar sin pena, pedir perdón,
sin que nuestro orgullo
o el ego se dañaría, o si pudieras decir
a tí mismo te perdono porque
te has portado muy mal pero
contigo mismo, porque es fácil
perdonar personas que te importan
pero el problema es perdonarse
a sí mismo, decirte te perdono, porque
uno mira los defectos de los demás,
pero mirarse sus defectos y perdonarlos
es muy difícil, pero traten compañeros
que se les hará fácil al final.

If a man could . . .
cry without shame, ask forgiveness,
without our pride
or ego getting hurt, or if you could say
to yourself I forgive you because
you've behaved badly, but
to yourself, because it's easy
to forgive people of importance to you,

the tricky thing is to forgive
yourself, to say to yourself I forgive you, because
one sees the defects of others,
but to see your own and forgive them
is very hard, but try, friends,
It will be easy in the end.

Written by a particularly sensitive and perceptive boy named Dariel, the poem stands as a remarkable gesture of heartfelt generosity: it is a gift of encouragement from one hurting child to his hurting peers. The poem also mentions the violence wrought sometimes by enforced conventions, which is to say that the poem might remind us, too, that we can change our immigration system. Its conventions are grounded in laws that we can rewrite, laws that are currently hurting people, including children. And that legal infrastructure is not a divine mandate; it was engineered by people and we the people can change it. We can develop and implement new policies and protocols to treat migrating people and refugees with dignity.

The children are especially powerful advocates of this message. I say this with tremendous confidence and hope after years of touring the United States and world to share their work and vision with thousands of diverse people. I have done this predominantly through presentations of the children's bilingual anthology of their poetry, which we together titled *Dreaming America: Voices of Undocumented Youth in Maximum-Security Detention*. It features forty-one of their poems, culled from workshops spanning from 2015 to 2017, and it stands importantly as the first ever book to be composed entirely by and of the voices of undocumented children in detention. Besides being an empowering triumph for its authors, many of whom had never even owned a book before, much less appeared in one, the book has proven important to its readers.

For example, as I traveled to share it, I learned just how few people had ever heard directly from a child in immigration detention, however often those same people in the audience might have read about, debated, and voted on policy affecting the children's lives.

In other words, too often the general public in the United States, and especially people in positions of power, have spoken about and for the children without ever including them in those conversations, despite the fact that those conversations determine their lives and futures. Consequently, such conversations leave intact all kinds of misconceptions and misinformation, and they end up causing terrible suffering and danger, up to and including death, whether by suicide or by murder. This was the case, for example, with the aforementioned boy from our workshop who was forcibly repatriated and then assassinated, exactly as he had predicted in court in his plea for the safety of asylum here.

In contradistinction to debates devoid of these children's voices, their poetry has paradoxically projected their voices from isolation into the public domain. There it has opened many minds and hearts around the country and world to new ways that we might live together in the age of climate change and mass migration.

Readers of *Dreaming America* have been inspired to become immigration attorneys, determined to fight for democracy and human rights through our legal system. Similarly, *Dreaming America* has inspired students to become bilingual family physicians and graduate students on doctoral programs studying migration and carcerality. *Dreaming America* has also inspired two original plays, an exhibition of original oil paintings in response to the poetry, and original music by at least four different composers. It also has inspired countless people to write responses to it, and to make their own, artful books by hand. Additionally, *Dreaming America* has also been assigned in countless schools at every educational level from junior high classes to Ph.D. programs.

This success is uniquely helpful not only for the exponentially growing circuitry of connections and discourse being generated on the topic of immigration, but also because profits from the sale of the book go to a legal defense fund for incarcerated undocumented children. In other words, the book is helping children to write their way to freedom. And I mention all of these examples as both encouraging indicators of the power of these incarcerated poets to connect with the public on a crucial issue, and as heartening examples of just how eager and ready we are as human beings to change our malignant immigration system.

To pursue such change, we must also work to understand how and why we have our current system. After all, if we are not a viciously sadistic people, and I do not think that we are, then why does our immigration system operate in our names as if we were?

More deeply, what is at stake in our policies and debates over family separation is nothing less than the very definition of who among us is human. This is nothing new to US discourses on immigration. To the contrary, such definitions have conditioned the very grounds of US history. Upon arrival here, the earliest (migrating) Europeans deemed Indigenous people subhuman. That disposition would be codified into the first US immigration law, the Naturalization Act of 1790, which offered citizenship only to white people of Western European origin. Forty years later, with the Indian Removal Act of 1830, Indigenous people were further dehumanized, stripped of their land, and forced to migrate under threat of death from the US military. And with the Civil Rights Act of 1866, which is the first US law to define citizenship, the nation in essence legislatively excluded its Indigenous people from belonging.

Such xenophobic and racist madness would persist in US policy well into the twentieth century. For example, in 1958 the United States implemented the Indian Adoption Project (IAP) to deal with what it termed the "Indian Problem." Here again, then, we see a federal project hinging on dehumanization, displacement, and family separation.

In practice, the IAP created a framework for the US government to separate roughly one-third of Indigenous children from their families. It then placed roughly 90 percent of those children in non-Indigenous homes. And this schematic for forced assimilation represents yet another attempt in US history by the federal government at white-nationalist ethnic cleansing.

Importantly herein, the IAP was lawful because Indigenous children were not legible as human beings in the eyes of the law. That legibility would only come with the passage in Congress of the Indian Child Welfare Act of 1978.

Sadly, there is currently no such legal defense of the humanity of migrating children in the United States. Consequently, the children in our poetry workshops, for example, remain illegible to the federal government. In practice, this results in a system that lawfully treats them as less than human. For if we as a nation could see Iván, the thirteen-year-old author of the following poem, as a human being, and as a human *child* at that, then how could we knowingly and intentionally keep him separated from his mother?

A mi madre
tu eres esa persona que
haces mi vida mejor,
siempre que te veo,
me alegras el corazón

tus labios son rojos
como una manzana
que me endulza
todas las mañanas

tus ojos son brillantes
como unos diamantes
súper gigantes

tu eres lo mejor
que me ha pasado
te amo mamá.

To My Mother
you're that person that
makes my life better,
whenever I see you,
you make my heart happy

your lips are red
as an apple
that sweetens me
each morning

your eyes shine
like supergiant
diamonds

you're the best thing
that's ever happened to me
I love you mom.

~~~

CHAPTER 11

We the People

I am cognizant of the interrelatedness of all communities
and states. I cannot sit idly by.

— DR. MARTIN LUTHER KING, JR.

I t's not manipulative. It's not hyperbolic. It's not dishonest
or propagandistic. It's not theoretical, fantastical, radical,
impractical, or even controversial. To the contrary, this book
is commonsensical, practical, and feasible. It's also benign,
vanilla. It's a simple call for the US government to treat all
people with dignity, as is already the will of the vast majority
of the American people.

Such a call for dignity may sound facile to readers, but
its absence from our immigration policy is causing undue
suffering. In other words, we are knowingly hurting human
beings daily with an immigration system that ignores their
basic humanity. I say that after having witnessed it exten-
sively in person for years, and also after having studied it
intensively throughout my decades-long academic career.
And while that action and study has most often been harsh
and dispiriting with its revelations of violence, misery, and
agony, it also has flashed with hope. And that hope is the
focus of this chapter.

Herein, however surprisingly, I'll share many causes for hope in the struggle to transform our immigration system, and thereby our nation. One of the most powerful among them lies in the fact that we as a nation already believe in what I'm proposing: we believe in the dignity of all human beings. And we can invoke that belief as the organizing principle of our reconception of our immigration system.

Currently, our immigration system is lacking in that principle. The system does not recognize the dignity of all people, however much that's one of our core values as the American people. If the system did believe in the dignity of all people, then it wouldn't preemptively cage people. It wouldn't imprison unaccompanied children, nor refuse them proper healthcare, education, or legal aid. It wouldn't create facilities to incarcerate mothers with their young children. Nor would it attack people by gender and sexuality, whether in the form of depriving girls and women of sanitary napkins, performing hysterectomies without consent, or putting trans women in cages with men. Nor would it perform such ghoulish violations of human rights as intentionally separating families by gender and age, and intentionally taking children from their parents, both of which are, incidentally, acts that the US government has at times sanctioned as federal policy dating back to the days of transatlantic slavery.

In short, were we to honor the dignity of all people, then our immigration system wouldn't perform such violences. Sadly, though, the system *is* doing all those violences, and more. Such is our policy. It's by design. We are intentionally denying the humanity of migrating people and refugees. It allows us to rationalize our violence against them. After all, if they're not fully human, then we needn't respect their basic human dignity.

But there is hope. Our immigration system is not some immutable truth delivered to us from the heavens to be unquestioningly, blindly followed. Rather it is something we've created, something we've made, and as such, it can be unmade, especially where urgently necessary. On top of that, we live in a representative democracy, meaning our elected officials are supposed to enact the will of the majority of the people. And the will of that majority is good. I see it clearly every time I travel the country to discuss immigration reform. The first questions during every question-and-answer session are "How is this happening?" and "How can I help?" In other words, the US public is as betrayed by its political representatives as it is concerned with the compassionate treatment of all people. We the people believe in the equality and dignity of all human beings.

Accordingly, there is everywhere a willingness to work for humane change in our immigration policy, and independent polls and academic studies reinforce my impression of our national character. I'll explain this in detail later in this chapter, but for now it's important to note that on the subject of immigration, we are not a nation fissured with divisions. We are not the racist and violent people that our immigration system might suggest, or that a minority of extremist leaders— from both major US political parties—might wish to push us to be. To the contrary, we are overwhelmingly unified in our belief in the value of immigration to our nation.

Perhaps even more encouragingly, we can do this through our individual strengths and skills, which are many and powerful. We are not helpless. We each can help in our own ways to promote meaningful change through our training, access, and expertise. This might come through politics, law, education, healthcare, economics, art, engineering, or other-wise, and it might course through our professional work or our volunteering. The opportunities are limited only by our respective imaginations, and we are a bright, creative, diverse, and skilled amalgamation of people. And within that vibrant mosaic of our national population, we each are an agent of transformation, and there is hope in that truth.

Concomitantly, while it's encouraging to note our individual potential, which is the potential of the human anywhere to create and endure, it bears immediate mention, too, that the deepest, most virulent problems within our immigration system are structural and systemic, not individual or personal. And that structure from its inception has systemized violence. When formulating our first federal immigration system in the late nineteenth century, we as a nation opted to root it in xenophobia.

That terrible decision continues to reverberate today, like a recurrent earthquake. I'll examine it in detail in a moment, but for now, in brief, it's important to understand that we poisoned our well upon building it, and we're yet to cleanse the water, and it's been almost one hundred and fifty years.

Perhaps that's because xenophobia is part and parcel of human nature. Perhaps it's natural to be uncomfortable with what's new and different. Perhaps it's normal to be suspicious of new people, though I'd prefer to think it isn't. What's certain, though, is that even if xenophobia is intrinsic to the human condition, it needn't be the organizing principle for an immigration system. And when it is the organizing principle, it guarantees violence. It is guaranteed to cause pain and suffering. How could it be otherwise, born as it is of a posture of anxious belligerence towards the arrival of new people?

Historically, we can date our immigration system back at least to 1875, when the US Supreme Court first declared immigration a federal issue. That Supreme Court decision established an opportunity to devise a thoughtful and just national immigration system. Instead what followed was an angry storm of xenophobic laws passed by Congress. That flawed federal start included such laws as the Chinese

Exclusion Act of 1882, which enacted a ten-year moratorium on immigration by Chinese laborers; the Immigration Act of 1882, which targeted migrating people as mentally incapable; and the Alien Contract Labor Law of 1885, which aimed to exclude working-class people from the country. And it is not hard to hear echoes of those discriminatory policies today.

Our immigration policies have continued to target people by race, ethnicity, and class. A good example is Title 42. It was initiated by President Donald Trump in March 2020 and continued by President Joe Biden until May 2023. Title 42 rejected impoverished migrating people and refugees at the Mexico-US border on the grounds that they represented a health risk to the United States during the COVID pandemic. However, this quite clearly stands in direct contradistinction to our treatment of tourists and workers arriving at that same border. More than 122 million of them crossed it into the United States in 2021 on buses, on trains, in trucks, in cars, and on foot.[1] When Title 42 was terminated, it was not by executive or legislative action. It was terminated by judicial review, with a humane federal judge in Washington, D.C., Emmet Sullivan, offering a precedent-setting determination that the policy was not only an unlawful violation of administrative procedure, but also "arbitrary and capricious."

Another of these modern, xenophobic policies that discriminates against people from certain countries of origin is the so-called Migrant Protection Protocols (MPP). Like Title 42, it was also begun under President Trump, albeit earlier, in January 2019. And like Title 42, it continued under President Biden until its judicial termination in October 2021. Despite the name, the Migrant Protection Protocols were by no means intended to protect migrating people or refugees. Rather, they target impoverished people via country of origin and funnel them into a punishing, indefinite process in Mexico along the border with the United States.

That process has spawned refugee camps there, trapping people in squalid, dangerous conditions, where they suffer violence, neglect, exposure, hunger, and despair.[2] In that regard, MPP partakes in the theatrical spectacle of cruelty that is the hallmark of the US immigration policy known as Prevention Through Deterrence.[3] That sadistically xenophobic policy has been favored by Congress and the White House since its inception in 1994 under President Bill Clinton.

For clarity's sake, though, we ought not simply juxtapose the nineteenth-century origins of the xenophobia in our federal immigration system with twenty-first-century reverberations in our current system. Rather, we should illuminate the system's pathway from its inception to the present. Such work reveals an unbroken thread of xenophobia running across the entire institutional history of our immigration system.

The benefits of tracing that history are at least twofold. First, in seeing clearly our institutional history, we might better understand how we've ended up today with a violent system that rationalizes taking children from parents, separating families by gender and age, incarcerating mothers with young children, and putting unaccompanied children in cages. Second, with that newfound understanding, we can better see how, why, and where we must change the system. We can speak with a confidence and insight born of the deep, factual understanding of our system's emergence and function.

In other words, with greater historical perspective, we can see that those aforementioned violences against migrating people and refugees were not the sudden and surprising consequence of a white-supremacist US president flexing his power unilaterally. Rather, they were symptomatic of the cancer of xenophobia that has afflicted our immigration system since its earliest years.

Since those early laws of the 1880s, we have been more or less stuck in a bog. The targets of emphasis have shifted with the political winds, but we have basically maintained xenophobic federal immigration policy across three centuries. For example, from our initial flurry of anti-Chinese and "anti-alien" legislation, we continued throughout the remainder of the nineteenth century to focus on wages in that policy. More precisely, our debates on immigration law and policy focused on the nativist regulation of wages in relation to the arrival and/or exclusion of migrating people. That focus on labor and wages was in fact so pronounced that it led the Bureau of Immigration to be relocated in 1903 from the Treasury Department to the Department of Commerce and Labor.

With the eruption of World War I, our focus shifted from wage regulation to questions of national origin. Accordingly, Congress passed a squall of laws like the Immigration Act of 1917, which explicitly banned Asian people and other non-white people from entering the United States. That act was subsequently fortified by the Immigration Acts of 1921 and 1924, which established explicit quotas for migrating people according to country of origin, again excluding all Asian people, and allotting almost all available spots to white Western and Northern European people.

In this manner Congress incrementally intensified its colorist endorsement of a white-supremacist biological determinism, meaning members continued to think and legislate according to the discriminatory belief that human potential was predetermined and limited by the color of one's skin, as well as the country of one's birth. And that virulent strain of xenophobia set precedents that continue to afflict our nation today.

Likewise, we continue to struggle with the consequences of the xenophobic origins of the creation in 1924 of the US Border

Patrol. It was conceived largely in response to national outrage that Mexican laborers had been exempted from the whites-only quota system of the recent immigration acts. Employers in the southwestern United States had vigorously fought for those exemptions. Congress negotiated a kind of compromise with the public, attempting to balance national xenophobia with localized labor needs, a theme subsequently pervading the history of our immigration system and our debates about it.

In this instantiation of that debate, Congress created the US Border Patrol within the Immigration Bureau of the Department of Labor. It was charged with securing US land borders between inspection stations. The first stations were opened in Detroit, Michigan, in June of 1924, and in El Paso, Texas, one month later. In 1925, Border Patrol agents began to patrol the seacoasts, too, but their early work proved uneven and irregular.

There were frequent complaints of mismanagement, abusive force, and haphazard regulation. Consequently, in 1932, the institution was split into two directorates, with one for the US border with Mexico, and the other for the border with Canada. And to this day we see asymmetrical narratives and processes for those two land borders, often for racialized, xenophobic reasons.

The next momentous change to our immigration system came in 1933 with the formation of Immigration and Natural-ization Services (INS). As aforementioned, World War I had triggered a major shift in focus by Congress from the regulation of wages to the regulation of bodies. The INS would accen-tuate this shift by helping Congress to focus increasingly on US borders by regulating the arrival of migrating people.

This transitioned into an ever more violent and paranoid xenophobia in Congress and the White House, which prior-itized more and more the use of the Border Patrol and INS to screen for the arrival of "enemy aliens." This included the creation of policies for the intensified policing of borders, and a series of internal, domestic campaigns designed to identify, detain, and deport Mexican people. Those sweeping, racist roundups were known as "repatriation," a process by which state and local governments, backed by the Border Patrol and INS, deported some 2 million people between 1929–1936, with as many as 1.2 million of them being US citizens.[4] Such was the fear of "enemies of the state," and it would only increase during the buildup to World War II.

For example, in June of 1939, in a fit of delirious xenophobia, the United States infamously refused asylum to the 937 refugees on the German ship *St. Louis* in port in Miami.[5] The government's grounds for the refusal were that the refugees were a threat to national security. Almost all of those refugees were Jewish, and more than a quarter of them were summarily murdered upon being returned to Nazi Germany.

During the war, our xenophobia only worsened. The federal government turned again on its own people. In an especially egregious example, President Franklin D. Roosevelt issued an executive order in 1942 to create internment camps for Japanese and Japanese American people, as well as a smaller number of German and Italian Americans. In all, roughly 120,000 US citizens were incarcerated in these prison camps. They were dehumanized, starved, and humiliated, and they suffered from a lack of healthcare, education, and housing. They also lost a collective $400 million dollars in property.[6] And they stand as yet another stark instantiation of xenophobia being wielded by those in power as their preferred tool to define who does and does not belong in the nation.

After our appalling xenophobia during World War II, and despite the war being over, we not only maintained our posture of anxiety and fear over migrating people as enemies of the state—we intensified it. For example, while our first major postwar immigration act, the Displaced Persons Act, was signed into law by President Harry Truman in 1948 and offered citizenship to select European refugees, it was annulled within four years by the Immigration and Nationality Act of 1952. Through that act, we intentionally reaffirmed discriminatory aspects of the 1917 and 1924 Immigration Acts, including a reassertion of a racialized quota system for migrating people. This time it earmarked 85 percent of the quotas for Western European people.

Concurrently, we expanded the authority of the Border Patrol to include the ability to detain and arrest people anywhere in the United States for being undocumented, and not only along the borders. We likewise empowered Border Patrol agents to search any vehicle anywhere for undocumented people. Such was the fervor of our xenophobia and our race-based fear of internal enemies.

Only in 1965 would Congress finally pass its first race-neutral immigration law, with the Immigration and Nationality Act. But that didn't mean our government had vanquished xenophobia. Rather, Congress had simply shifted again the focus of its xenophobia, this time from race to poverty. In practice, this meant the government prioritized the issuance of short- and long-term visas to skilled laborers and investors over working and impoverished people and refugees.

That xenophobic focus on poverty would continue for decades. For example, the Immigration Reform and Control Act of 1986 targeted undocumented people working in menial labor. It was premised on the wrongheaded presupposition that impoverished, migrating people were the cause of domestic and international inequality, and not a consequence of it. Nevertheless, this wrongheaded thinking translated into the infamous period of mass raids by US Border Patrol agents of US factories, restaurants, construction sites, businesses, and elsewhere. Under INS authority, armed agents would burst in unannounced, hoping to find, detain, and deport undocumented people, all the while disrupting commerce and spreading fear, paranoia, and instability in the name of justice, well-being, and stability.

It seems important to note here, too, that impoverished people were migrating to the United States from nations where the United States had often gone first. In other words, the United States had for decades gone into other nations around the world to recruit labor via extractive, colonial logics, and that created the binational pathways that many migrants were now traveling.

A good example of this comes in the Bracero Program that President Roosevelt initiated by executive order in 1942. It was created not six months after Roosevelt's creation of the Japanese internment camps that led to the labor shortage that the Bracero Program aimed to fix. It reached into Mexico to recruit more than 4.5 million farm workers between 1942–1964, and those Mexican farmworkers in turn used their knowledge, sweat, and skill to help to build California's agrarian economy into a global powerhouse in itself.[7]

Meanwhile, our federal immigration policies continued to target impoverished people as the enemies of the state, and our next momentous change to our immigration system came in the early 1990s with the introduction of the strategy known officially as Prevention Through Deterrence.[8] The strategy aimed to deter migrating people and refugees from crossing the Mexico-US border. To that end, the strategy emphasized the theatrical use of cruelty not only to punish people for migrating without proper paperwork, but also to discourage others from ever attempting to migrate.

Born of a deeply cynical xenophobia, this strategy would quickly prove to be as deadly as it was vicious. To maintain the aim of frightening away newcomers, advocates of this strategy would rather see migrating people die in the desert as a warning to any future traveler, than offer migrating people and refugees in need any assistance, not even water. In fact, Border Patrol agents have been known to slash open containers of water left by good samaritans in the desert for dehydrated migrating people. Consequently, Prevention Through Deterrence has officially led to more than 10,000 deaths in the Sonoran Desert alone since 1994. Some nongovernmental groups estimate that total to be as high as 80,000 people,[9] though such figures are hard to determine with precision due to the harshness of the landscape.[10]

More specifically, many human corpses go unrecovered and uncounted because they disappear so quickly in the desert, often within forty-eight hours. This is due to myriad factors including the scorching sun, which can regularly spike temperatures to over 110 degrees Fahrenheit; the scarcity of water; the scarcity of food; the rugged topography, in which people routinely lose their way; fourteen species of rattlesnake; and predatory animals like vultures that disarticulate, skeletonize, and even completely disappear human remains. It is a gruesome system that subjects human beings to excruciating suffering and death. And to knowingly subject desperate people, including refugees, to such trauma in itself is another stark, sad reminder of the lack of recognition of the dignity of all people, including our own, which we besmirch. In other words, what do we become in performing and even cheering on this macabre cruelty?

Unfortunately, this system remains our current strategy. It has failed now for decades, and at a tremendous human, ethical, political, and economic cost. Besides its catastrophic failure in bioethical terms as a policy of deadly sadism, the strategy has failed in that it has not achieved its stipulated aim. It has not deterred migration. There were roughly 1 million undocumented people in the United States in 1990, 3 million people in 2000, 6 million people in 2010, and 10 million people in 2020.[11] Today, the number is somewhere around 13 million people.[12] In other words, Prevention Through Deterrence is not deterring people from migrating.

On top of that, our failed strategy of Prevention Through Deterrence has increasingly gorged on taxpayer money over the past three decades. For example, according to the American Immigration Council (AIC), from 1993 to 2021, the annual federal budget for the US Border Patrol skyrocketed from $362.66 million US dollars to $19.6 billion US dollars.[13] Similarly, the federal budget for ICE has grown exponentially since its inception. According to ICE itself, the agency received a $3.3 billion US dollar budget for its first year, 2003, and that budget had tripled to approximately $9.5 billion US dollars by 2024.[14] Moreover, in total, since 2003, we are estimated by congressional appropriations bills for fiscal years 2004–2024 to have spent more than $409 billion dollars on immigration enforcement by the end of 2024.[15] For such a formidable concentration of money, resources, time, and legislation, we ought by now to have a far better system. At the very least, it should stand for the values and beliefs of the American people and treat all people with dignity as they filter through it.

While focusing on the management of Prevention Through Deterrence, we've been ignoring the factors that drive people to immigrate in the first place. They include climate change, economic inequality, poverty, and corruption.[16] These are among the issues that we should be addressing robustly through our immigration debates and legislation. None of them will be resolved by a US immigration policy that focuses on militarizing borders and caging migrating people.

If we truly want to diminish migration, then we must address the conditions that spawn it. Again, very few people choose to migrate, and no one chooses to be a refugee. Rather, they are driven to it by desperation, suffering, and violence. Additionally, the subsequent life of an exile in a new land is always streaked with some degree of sorrow and struggle due to the difficulties of displacement and loss.

Accordingly, we ought to invest our time, attention, and resources into thinking of ways to help people to avoid that trauma. One option is to help to stabilize the region and planet. I am thinking, for example, of climate change. By making life more sustainable for people everywhere, we help to diminish the pressure to migrate. We help people to stay in their families, their homes, their cultures, their languages, and their countries, as most people wish.

If left unchecked, climate change will continue to worsen and will intensify the pressure on millions of people to migrate. For example, climate change has caused a spike in the intensity and frequency of natural disasters, and they correlate to spikes in displacement and migration. We've seen this recently with Hurricanes Eta and Iota, for instance, which ravaged Honduras, Nicaragua, and Guatemala in but two weeks in 2020. They affected more than 7.5 million people and caused a surge in migration across those nations.[17] And people all over the world are being similarly forced to migrate by the destruction of their homelands and natural resources, including such basic necessities for life as arable land and water.

Thus, green policies should form a crucial component of any humane immigration reform. Moreover, concerns over environmental destruction are inextricably linked with concerns over poverty. Today, more than 1 billion people in the world lack access to water, and that number is projected to escalate dramatically in the coming decades, in part due to climate change. Additionally, roughly 8.5 percent of the world's population, some 700 million people, currently live in extreme poverty, earning less than $2.15 per day.[18] Without water and/or without money for basic necessities, how are people to live in an ever more volatile global climate?

Already vast swaths of the world's population are suffering from deprivation, pain, and uncertainty, and more people are migrating today than ever before, and by a dramatic margin. To wit, according to the United Nations Department of Economic and Social Affairs, which issues comprehensive and definitive global analyses of migration every five years, there were roughly 153 million people migrating around the world in 1990, and that number jumped to 281 million people in 2020.[19] That number is projected to continue to rise with the 2025 report if we keep to our current course, with ever more people migrating to avoid dying of hunger.

But as suggested throughout this chapter, there are reasons for hope. We don't have to live like this. We in the States are not resigned to our immigration system as is. We think globally and act locally, as the saying goes, by acting for environmental protection and by acting to eradicate income inequality and poverty. We also can act for the ethical treatment of all human beings in our care, and we can reach out to other nations and organizations to create bilateral, informed, reasonable, and sustainable opportunities to collaborate on creating more security for all people wherever they wish to live.

Along those lines, one powerful, feasible, and free activity that we each can engage in on the subject of immigration reform is the work of debunking of xenophobic mistruths about migrating people and refugees. Such mistruths often invoke dehumanizing and demonizing language to degrade and misrepresent people so that harm can be done to them, often with impunity.

Simply flip on right-wing news and you'll soon hear the kind of language and mistruths I'm referring to. There the newscasters, politicians, and/or guests don't hesitate to call migrating people criminals, for example. More precisely, you'll hear them called rapists, thieves, drug lords, gangsters, grifters, derelicts, and terrorists. They want them held in detention centers like prisoners of war for "invading" the United States. They fearmonger over invading hordes, which they conjure as advancing "caravans" of criminals, brutes, ignoramuses, and mooches. Nor do they care if those migrating people are mistreated while in our care. They simply want them erased from our landscape, which is a classic wish of fascist imaginations everywhere and across all time. That's why they dream and speak of such themes as purity and homogeneity, though no such things exist, not even within their ranks—or even their own bodies.

In other words, those xenophobic people not only air their ignorance by spewing their dehumanizing language, they also threaten democracy itself with their fascist ideals. And against such attempted subversion of our democratic values, we can work to debunk their mistruths.

Individually, this will require each of us to act for change, and collectively, we as constituents of a representative democracy can foment systemic changes. We can learn and share credible information, and we can advocate for our elected officials to represent our values and beliefs.

Our current system is destroying people daily. It is suspending, deforming, and even ending their lives. But we can change that. Our system can be rewritten. Violence no longer needs to be perpetrated in our names and against our ethics. We are not a nation of violent xenophobes. Let us work together to prove this to the people currently suffering in our immigration system, as well as to ourselves and to one another.

~~~~~

Epilogue:
To the Children
in Detention

Dear Children,

Please forgive me. I've failed you, as has my nation.

Here this morning, as I walk in sunshine through the woods behind my home, I'm thinking of you. Your voices. Your faces.

I feel so grateful to have known you, and so terribly sad about why and where.

My greatest hope is that today you are free.

I hope you're living where and how you wish, though I doubt it. I know the politics, the courts, the money in your captivity.

It also makes me think about the ways our paths through life preexist us.

I was raised 2,500 miles from here. You hail from disparate points even further away. Yet here we are, intertwined, our braided paths running through this ancient valley.

The geologists tell us that these mountains date back at least half a billion years. You'd be moved by their timeless beauty. And you wouldn't be alone in those feelings.

It stirs the imaginations of locals and visitors alike. Most can't help but pull out cell phones and snap photos. Strong is the human wish to remember how beautiful the world can be.

It's why people write songs about this place and paint its landscapes. It's why others set their novels here, or their weddings, or their homesteads. And you wouldn't believe the number of hikers who pass through.

Speaking of passers-through, you should know, too, that people have been migrating through this valley for at least 15,000 years.

Currently, as we've discussed in workshop, it's considered rural Virginia.

Culturally, it's Southern, meaning stilted, bellicose, and amnesiac. Confederate flags snap angrily over land once Monacan and Manahoac. Here enslaved people were first forced into the colonies in 1619, but there's more statuary honoring murderous traitors and slavers than the enslaved people who built the United States into a global power. Here there are more churches than schools. Here there are more places to buy and shoot guns than there are food banks and soup kitchens, this despite a whopping 39 percent of our households earning less than the cost of living, meaning they can't make ends meet.

Sometimes I wonder if the beauty of the world is wasted on human beings.

But then I think of you.

You're the beauty we aspire to be.

You're shining examples of what individual humans can achieve.

You're bright with creativity, kindness, courage, generosity, and resilience.

It's how you survived your childhoods, how you traversed nations, and how you fight for better futures.

If more of us moved through foreign countries alone as young teens—never mind doing it penniless, targeted, and desperate—how might we learn to treat newcomers to our communities differently?

I love you for your minds. They glitter like diamonds under a full moon, spraying flashes of color into the surrounding darkness.

And I love the exquisite maps you've designed in your minds to lead your lustrous futures. I hope those plans come true, and soon.

That is, I hope you'll soon be free.

Once you are, never forget this truth: you're a gift to any community you join. They're lucky to have you.

And I hope you'll raise your voices there where you resettle. Your poetry alone is proof of your wisdom and goodwill.

In short, you're beautiful people. Don't let xenophobes or bigots lead you to believe anything different.

I mean, how many of us can honestly claim that each day we're working to transform our suffering into our dreams?

You're each an inspiration.

Remember that wherever and however you're living.

And you're not an inspiration because you're unique or exceptional. No, you're an inspiration because you've undertaken the hard work of striving to explore what's too often left latent in the human condition: the capacity within each of us to see and seek a safer, kinder world for all of us to partake in.

That's why I've repeatedly told you in workshop that you're harbingers of a crucial hope.

You represent a mode of listening to others with patience, focus, and empathy.

You exemplify that every time you welcome what's new, different, and even a little scary.

In that manner you lead us towards ways of living more fully together, enriched by our dissimilarities, not fearing them.

It's why I believe you could inspire this nation to recover its wayward soul.

Your presence here is the gift of that opportunity.

But the gift is wasted. We refuse it.

We turn our backs on the new and different. We let fear blind us to opportunity.

For instance, almost everyone living here is a monolingual English speaker. That makes your presence here a linguistic gift. Sadly, though, we plug our ears to the beauty of the languages you've brought with you. We intentionally silence Spanish, Mam, Náhuatl, *Q'anjob'al*, Mixtec, and many other rich and vibrant ways of thinking, sharing, and being.

It's a willful insistence on provincial ignorance.

We could be living a shimmering linguistic rainbow instead of a falsely monochromatic smear.

Worse still, we lock you—children!—away in concrete cells in our midst.

We fill your lungs with stale air, not the local mountain breezes. We poison your minds with ideas of us as a nation of raging sadists.

Our judges become the vengeful demigods of a minority of racists.

Our armed guards become your de facto parents. You, who are children in our care. You, who we never let feel the sun on your skin.

Still, even locked down in detention, you find ways to crack each other up.

Great upwellings of laughter from deep in your bellies, your hearts, erupt every time I visit. Pealing laughter heard in workshop. Through concrete walls. Through solid steel doors.

It resounds through raw conversations about migration and detention, and through blinding blizzards of depression. Warm, shared laughter like a powerful hug from a friend when you're afraid, tearful, or melancholic.

It affirms that you're loved in this world, even when you're most desperately doubting it.

Yes, you have that magic: you know how to manufacture strength. You know how to mine pain for love.

You create sparks of light inside a dark tomb, whether with a quip, a song, a drawing, a poem, or a few tender, uplifting words whispered to a suffering peer.

And just like that, there it is: a perfect yellow tulip growing from the smooth concrete floor of an isolation cell.

How I cherish those memories of your resilience, your hope, your compassion, and your creativity.

They demonstrate how love is insistent and can bloom anywhere, even in detention centers.

When you're free, that lone tulip will become a prairie full of colorful flowers.

What I'm trying to say is that you sustain one another, against all odds and through tremendous pain.

And you sustain me too. I'm so profoundly grateful to you. In trying moments, you're often there with me. When I'm worried over a surgery, a bill, or one of my sons at yet another new school, a memory of you will resurge, and I'll hear your voices, see your faces, recall your wisdom.

I'll hear Saúl reading softly to Edgar through his cell door and helping him to write a poem while Edgar's in lockdown and therefore barred from workshop for the week.

I'll watch Roberto sidle over to Dante unprompted to scribe for him, because Dante has a poem in his heart but never learned to write or read and so needs help to get it onto paper.

I'll witness Carlos at the start of workshop cradling Santos's bandaged wrists after another suicide attempt, and then I'll hear Carlos read aloud Santos's poem to the group because he couldn't get through it himself, the tears too choking.

Such staggering kindness. I have no right to have witnessed it. None of us adults out here do.

It's the kind of compassion that emerges in the precious intimacy among children facing fierce adversity, ablaze with all of the beauteous innocence and optimism of youth.

But how long can it hold out? How much are we demanding of you, we adults who could change the conditions of your lived experience?

How often do we adults look away from the suffering because it's easier for us not to face it, even as we know it's being done, and in our names?

But not you.

You children give and give to one another, even while fighting for your very right each to exist.

You who make friends and speak of love and design beautiful futures while shackled and chained.

You who invert time: children teaching adults.

You who encourage us to open our hearts and grow and share.

You who show us how to live through compassion, determination, and inclusion.

And I, a poet who has published eighteen books, who has dedicated his very life to studying and sharing language, have no words to name my shame at the fact that my country cages refugee children.

We do it knowingly, on purpose, in the name of justice and community. What a farce. I'm so sorry that you suffer its terrible violence.

The shame shakes me to my core.

The shame mutes the natural beauty of these woods, this valley.

How to look my neighbors in the eye and wish them "Good morning" when they might be among those who'd have you caged and suffering in perpetuity?

Please believe me when I tell you that those who cheer for children to be caged are sick in their hearts. Their minds are diseased. Their lives will stand for all eternity as tributes to hatred and cruelty.

Thankfully, though, they're also a minority here. They're a small fraction of the national population of the United States.

Beyond Congress in its overwhelming power, and beyond the scattered dens of bigotry that blister and pockmark the country, our nation is so much more welcoming and compassionate than our federal immigration system would lead you to believe.

On the whole, our hearts are good, as are those of most human beings everywhere.

And speaking of hearts, I know yours. I know how much you're hurting.

I know it from your poetry.

I know it from our conversations.

I know it from your silences and scars.

I know it from your bandaged wrists and bruised throats.

I know it just as I know, too, that you'd thrive out here.

I know you'll flourish if freed and supported.

And I know you'd love this trail that I'm just now walking, thinking of you.

May your feet carry you away from concrete cellblocks and onto soft paths through life, like this one.

May your nose be filled with a sweet, gentle breeze, like the one just now blending clover, violets, and geraniums.

May your body soften with the relaxing warmth of this sunshine on your shoulders and faces.

May you remember with pride that this land has always been a corridor for migrating humans.

In other words, there is nothing unseemly or deficient in being a migrating person. That is what we human beings do.

I wish we could discuss this while walking these woods together. Or if you'd prefer, we could simply walk in silence.

Either way, silent or chatting, we'd be present in this radiant landscape, soaking in the beauty of being here, alive and free.

I know you'd find peace in these hills.

I know you'd find clarity and serenity.

I'm not saying you'd be healed, whether here or anywhere. Your spirit is scarred, and it always will be. But you needn't be ashamed of those scars, nor must you suffer them alone.

Here in these woods where I'm thinking of you, everything is wreathed in golden forsythia. Loops of powdery bluebells nod in the breeze, revealing the season.

It's spring. Life is succeeding in its struggle to resurface after wintry detention.

I hope some of that new life is yours.

I hope you emerge, bloom, and shine here in all of your beauty.

What a triumph that would be, for you, for all of us here.

~~~

Acknowledgments

My gratitude runs so deep for so many people, groups, and institutions that I am reluctant to try to express it here for fear of failing to mention everyone behind this sprawling, transnational collaboration. Please forgive me in advance any unintended exclusions, much as I beg you, too, to accept these few, meager words of thanks when each of you, including you, dear reader, deserves so much more. First and foremost, I wish to thank my sons, Ilan and Joaquín, for their love and brilliance, both in my life and in the world. I also must immediately thank each migrating person with whom I have worked in any capacity since childhood. I likewise thank my magnificent literary agent for making this book possible; my extraordinary editor, Fiona Hallowell; and also Marjorie Agosín; María Alcira Serna; Jimmy Santiago Baca; Bahir Al Badry; Juan Pablo Berrizbeitia; Florencia Diano Borghini; David Baluarte; Curtis Bauer; Claudia Bernardi; Mark Buller; Gabrielle Calvocoressi; Cristina Casado; Avery Chenoweth; Kristin Clarens; Nathan D.B. Connolly; Vicki Conti; David Coogan; Carmen Coury; Tanishka Cruz; Michael Cucher; Leandro Delgado; Arthur Dixon; Silvia Facal Santiago; Marco Fajardo; William Faraclas;

Ana María Fernández; Montserrat Feu López; Elisa Filippone; Renée Fleming; Nancy Maribel García García; Fiorela Giraldo Prado de Lewis; Irazú Gómez Vargas; Tammi Helwig; Juan Felipe Herrera; Jessica Ibañez Whitlock; Jessica Infanzon; Khizr Khan; Jessie Knadler; Agustín Labat; Rodger LeGrand; Linda Lerner; Adriana Libonati; Alexandra Lossada; Georgina Marie; Maria Mazziotti Gillan; Lulu Miller; Jacki Moffi; Larry Moffi; Angélica Morales Santiago; José Navarro; Omar Núñez Méndez; Facundo Ponce de León; Alicia Partnoy; Ricardo Preve; Anishka Sharma; Judith Shatin; Katie Shepherd; Daniel Simon; Jordan Smith; Jeremy Turner; Alicia Valentín Mendoza; Romina Casatti Velázquez; Patricia Vargas; Amanda Venta; Florence Weinberg; Lesley Wheeler; and Sister Maggie Yee. I likewise bow in thanks to the American Civil Liberties Union; American Immigration Council; American Immigration Lawyers Association; Angry Tías & Abuelas; BBC; Capital Area Immigrants' Rights Coalition; CASA; Catholic Legal Immigration Network; Charlottesville High School; Dilley Pro Bono Project; Florence Immigrant & Refugee Rights Project; Immigration Justice Campaign; Immigration Rescue Committee; Justice Arts Coalition; MANOS; National Public Radio; Raíces; Sin Barreras; Virginia Humanities; Welcoming Greater Charlottesville; Words Without Borders; and Washington and Lee University, particularly Dean Chawne Kimber, Provost Lena Hill, Dean Emeritus Suzanne Keen, the Office of General Counsel, my colleagues in Latin American and Caribbean Studies, my colleagues in Romance Languages, and my students, particularly those in "Poetry and Politics of Immigration," who accompanied me weekly to the juvenile immigration detention center for one semester and thereby began their own work for immigration reform and a better future for all.

~~~~~

Notes

Introduction

[1]This is an inherent right of all human beings according to the United Nations Convention Against Torture and Other Cruel, Inhuman or Degrading Treatment or Punishment (26 June 1987).

[2]Stevenson, Bryan. *Just Mercy: A Story of Justice and Redemption*. New York: One World, 2015. p 18.

[3]Mandela, Nelson. *The Prison Letters of Nelson Mandela*. Ed. Sahm Venter. New York: Liveright Publishing Corporation, 2018, p. 81.

[4]According to the United Nations Refugee Convention and its Optional Protocol, it is unlawful to treat people seeking asylum as criminals. See Convention and Protocol Relating to the Status of Refugees. United Nations, Office of the United Nations High Commissioner for Refugees. The 1951 Convention was created in New York and signed by the U.S. 28 July 1951, with the U.S. signing the subsequent, additional Protocol on 1 November 1968.

[5]MLK, *Strength to Love*. New York: Harper & Row, 1963. p. 72.

Chapter 1: So It Begins

[1]Wong, Kelsey R. "Written Statement by Kelsey R. Wong, Program Director, Shenandoah Valley Juvenile Center." Permanent Subcommittee on Investigations, Committee on Homeland Security and Governmental Affairs, United States Senate, 26 April 2018.

[2]Knadler, Jessie. "Inhumane Conditions Alleged at Juvenile Detention Center Near Staunton." WMRA, National Public. Radio. 13 December 2017;

Biesecker, Michael. "Young Immigrants Detained in Virginia Center Allege Abuse." AP News. 21 June 2018; Biesecker, Michael, Jake Pearson, and Garance Burke. "Governor Orders Probe of Abuse Claims by Immigrant Children." AP News. 21 June 2018; Biesecker, Michael. "Probe: Latino Teens Strapped Down at SVJC, but Not Abused." AP News. 13 August 2018; Washington Lawyers' Committee for Civil Rights and Urban Affairs. "Written Testimony to the U.S. Commission on Civil Rights Regarding the Condition of Immigrant Detention Centers and the Status of Treatment of Immigrant Children in Detention." 13 May 2019; United States District Court for the Western District of Virginia, Harrisonburg Division. *Doe v. Shenandoah Valley Juvenile Center Commission*, "Class Action Complaint," 5:17CV00097. 4 October 2017; United States District Court for the Western District of Virginia, Harrisonburg Division. *Doe v. Shenandoah Valley Juvenile Center Commission*, "Answer," 5:17CV00097. 3 November 2017; United States District Court for the Western District of Virginia, Harrisonburg Division. *John Doe 1, et al. by and Through Their Next Friend, Nelson Lopez, on Behalf of Themselves and All Persons Similarly Situated, Plaintiffs, v. Shenandoah Valley Juvenile Center Commission*, 5:17CV00097. 28 February 2018; United States Court of Appeals for the Fourth Circuit. *Doe 4 v. Shenandoah Valley Juvenile Center Commission*, No. 19-1910. 14 January 2021.

[3]Pearson, Jake. "Hope, Despair in Poetry by Immigrant Children in US Lockup." AP News. 21 June 2018; Michelson, Seth. *Dreaming America Voices of Undocumented Youth in Maximum-Security Detention*. Silver Springs: Settlement House, 2017: 100–101; Sanchez, Melissa, et al. "As Months Pass in Chicago Shelters, Immigrant Children Contemplate Escape, Even Suicide." ProPublica. 6 September 2018; Habib, Yamily. "Suicide and Despair: The Reality of Young Immigrants in Detention Centers." *Al Día*. 11 September 2018; Liebelson, Dana. "In Detention, Troubling Cases Of Self-Harm Among Migrant Youth." HuffPost. 3 August 2018; Sanchez, Melissa, et al. "As Months Pass in Chicago Shelters, Immigrant Children Contemplate Escape, Even Suicide." ProPublica. 6 September 2018; Erfani, Parsa, Elizabeth T. Chin, Caroline H. Lee, Nishant Uppal, and Katherine R Peeler. "Suicide rates of migrants in United States immigration detention (2010–2020)." AIMS Public Health. 8.3 (2021): 416–420.

[4]*Southwest Border Deaths by Fiscal Year*. US Border Patrol. 2024; "Southwest Border Deaths By Fiscal Year (1998–2000)." U.S. Border Patrol, Southwest Sector; "Fiscal Year 2021 Office of Professional Responsibility CBP-Related Deaths Report." U.S. Customs and Border Protection. 06 February 2023; "Fiscal Year 2022 Office of Professional Responsibility CBP-Related Deaths Report." U.S. Customs and Border Protection. 18 March 2024; Eschbach, Karl, Hagan, Jacqueline, Rodriguez, Nestor, Hernández-León, Rubén, and Bailey, Stanley. "Death at the border." *International Migration Review*. 1999; LoMonaco, Claudine. "Border Patrol: We'll Tally Dead Migrants Better." *Tucson Citizen*, 2005; Martinez, Daniel, et al. "A Continued Humanitarian Crisis on the Border: Undocumented Border Crossers Deaths Recorded by the Pima County Office of the Medical Examiner 1990–2012." Binational Migration Institute. Tucson: University of Arizona (2013); Martínez, Daniel E. et al. "Migrant Deaths in Southern Arizona: Recovered Undocumented Border

Crosser Remains Investigated by the Pima County Office of the Medical Examiner, 1990–2020." Binational Migration Institute, University of Arizona: 2021; Leutert, Stephanie. "The Border Patrol's Migrant Death Undercounting in South Texas." *Journal on Migration and Human Security* 12.3 (2024), 277–289.

[5]Office of Refugee Resettlement Annual Report to Congress 2014. U.S. Office of Refugee Resettlement, 2016.

[6]"Annual Report," Core Civic, SEC, 2020. https://ir.corecivic.com/node/21411/html; "Annual Report," The Geo Group, Inc., SEC, 2020, https://seekingalpha.com/filings/pdf/14711618; Hyunhye Cho, Eunice. "More of the Same: Private Prison Corporations and Immigration Detention Under the Biden Administration." American Civil Liberties Union. 5 October 2021; "Latest UC Data – FY2020." U.S. Department of Health and Human Services, 2020; Hyunhye Cho, Eunice, Tara Tidwell Cullen and Clara Long. *Justice-Free Zones U.S. Immigration Detention Under the Trump Administration.* American Civil Liberties Union, 2020; "Geo Group Inc., Form 10-K." U.S. Securities and Exchange Commission. 16 February 2021.

[7]Hyunhye Cho, Eunice. "More of the Same: Private Prison Corporations and Immigration Detention Under the Biden Administration." American Civil Liberties Union. 5 October 2021.

[8]Hyunhye Cho, Eunice. "Unchecked Growth: Private Prison Corporations and Immigration Detention, Three Years Into the Biden Administration." American Civil Liberties Union. 7 August 2023.

[9]Warren, Elizabeth and Alex Padilla. "Letter to DHS and ICE on Private Detention Center Use." U.S. Senate. 14 May 2024; "The Cost of Immigration Enforcement and Border Security." American Immigration Council. August 2024; "Budget Overview." Department of Homeland Security, U.S. Customs and Border Protection. 2025.

[10]"Policy Brief | Snapshot Of ICE Detention: Inhumane Conditions And Alarming Expansion." National Immigrant Justice Center. 20 September 2024.

Chapter 3: Looking for Light

[1]"Secretary Kirstjen M. Nielsen Announces Historic Action to Confront Illegal Immigration." Department of Homeland Security. 20 December 2018; "Migrant Protection Protocols." Department of Homeland Security. 24 January 2019; "Policy Guidance for Implementation of the Migrant Protection Protocols." Department of Homeland Security. 25 January 2019; UNHCR alarmed over US 'expulsion flights' to southern Mexico. United Nations. 11 August 2021; "The 'Migrant Protection Protocols': an Explanation of the Remain in Mexico Program." American Immigration Council. 12 February 2025.

[2]Althaus, Dudley. "Migrants Hunkered Down in Crowded, Filthy Border Encampment." 17 November 2019; Tucker, Brendon and Erin Hughes. *Notes*

from the Field: "México: Matamoros." Global Response Management. 2019; "Conditions in Matamoros Refugee Camp Put Children's Health and Safety at Risk." Young Center for Immigrant Children's Rights. 28 January 2020; Burnett, John. "A Migrant Father Sends His Son To The U.S.: 'I Know That He's Safe.'" National Public Radio. 9 March 2020; Hennessy-Fiske, Molly. "Joy, despair, uncertainty in migrant tent camp as Biden Policy Evolves." *Los Angeles Times*. 26 February 2021; Mercado A, Garcini L, Venta A, Paris M. "'Remain In Mexico': Stories of Trauma And Abuse." National Library of Medicine 40.7 (2021): 1170–1173; Cook, Christa. "Matamoros Refugee Camp II WASH Assessment." Solidarity Engineering. 12 January 2023. Bermudez Tapia, B. A. "From Matamoros to Reynosa: Migrant Camps on the U.S.-Mexico Border." *Contexts* 22.1 (2023): 30–37; Laughon K, Montalvo-Liendo N, Eaton S, Bassett L. "Health and safety concerns of female asylum seekers living in an informal migrant camp in Matamoros, Mexico." *Journal of Advanced Nursing* 79.5 (2023): 1830–1839; Bermúdez Tapia, Bertha A. "Migrant Camps, the Worsening of Violence, and the Erasure of Asylum." *Footnotes* (American Sociological Association) 51.3 (2023).

[3]Metering was determined to be illegal by the Ninth Circuit of the US federal court of appeals on 23 October 2024. See United States Court of Appeals for the Ninth Circuit. "Al Otro Lado v. Mayorkas." 23 October 2024.

[4]"Migrant Protection Protocols Cohort Reports." Office of Homeland Security Statistics. U.S. Department of Homeland Security.

[5]"CBP Enforcement Statistics." U.S. Customs and Border Protection.

[6]"Recommendations to End 'Remain in Mexico' and Bring People Seeking Protection Safely into the United States." Human Rights First, January 2021, p. 3.

[7]"Alien Protection Protocols FY 2020." U.S. Customs and Border Protection.

Chapter 4: Dilley

[1]Martinez Gina. "A Mother Says Her 19-Month-Old Daughter Died After Being Held by ICE. Now She's Suing for Millions." TIME. 29 August 2018.

[2]U.S. Department of Homeland Security. Office of the Inspector General. "Immigration and Customs Enforcement Did Not Follow Federal Procurement Guidelines When Contracting for Detention Services." 21 February 2018; "Cut the Contracts: It's Time to End ICE's Corrupt Detention Management System." National Immigration Justice Center. March 2021.

In December of 2021 ICE shifted the focus of the facility from family detention to the detention of single adults. ICE then terminated the contract with CoreCivic for the South Texas Family Residential Center, effective 9 August 2024. "Readout of US Immigration and Customs Enforcement visit to the South Texas Family Residential Center in Dilly, TX." U.S. Immigration and Customs Enforcement. 28 February 2024; "CoreCivic Receives Termination Notice From U.S. Immigration and Customs Enforcement At South Texas Family Residential Center." CoreCivic. 10 June 2024;

Williams, William. "CoreCivic Stock Takes Hit after ICE Center Closing Announcement." *Nashville Post*. 12 June 2024; Sanchez, Sandra. "ICE to Close Nation's Largest Migrant Detention Center in South Texas." News WKRG. 24 June 2024.

Chapter 6: Digital Activism: The Yin

[1]Eagly, Ingrid V. and Steven Shafer. "A National Study of Access to Counsel in Immigration Court." *University of Pennsylvania Law Review* 164.1 (December 2015): p. 50; Shah, Aditi and Eunice Hyunhye Cho. "No Fighting Chance: ICE's Denial of Access to Counsel in U.S. Immigration Detention Centers." ACLU Research Report. 9 June 2022. P. 5, 10.

[2]Eagly, Ingrid V. and Steven Shafer. "Measuring *In Absentia* Removal in Immigration Court." American Immigration Council, January 2021. P. 4; "11 Years of Government Data Reveal That Immigrants Do Show Up for Court." Press Release, American Immigration Council. 28 January 2021; "Fact Check: Asylum Seekers Regularly Attend Immigration Court Hearings." Human Rights First. January 2019.

Chapter 10: Harvested Fruit

[1]"Interagency Task Force on the Reunification of Families Interim Progress Report." U.S. Department of Homeland Security. 22 April 2024; Dickerson, Caitlin. "The Family-Separation Files." *The Atlantic*. 31 December 2022; Khardori, Ankush. "How America Forgot About One of Trump's Most Brutal Policies." Politico. 28 October 2024.

[2]Kraft, Colleen. "Separating Parents from Their Kids at the Border Contradicts Everything We Know About Children's Welfare." *Los Angeles Times*. 3 May 2018; López, Ana María. "ACP Objects to Separation of Children from their Parents at Border." American College of Physicians. 18 May 2018; "Statement of Hilarie Bass, ABA President Re: Separating Immigrant Children from Parents at the Border." American Bar Association. 30 May 2018; Shoichet, Catherine E. "Doctors Saw Immigrant Kids Separated from Their Parents. Now They're Trying to Stop It." CNN. 19 June 2018; Cumming-Bruce, Nick. "U.N. Rights Chief Tells U.S. to Stop Taking Migrant Children from Parents." *The New York Times*. 18 June 2018; Cheng, Amrit. "Fact-Checking Family Separation." American Civil Liberties Union. 19 June 2018; Karp, Brad S., and Gary M. Wingens. "The Law Did Not Create This Crisis, but Lawyers Will Help End It." *The New York Times*. 25 June 2018; Panduranga, Harsha. "Trump Admin's Distorted Data Doesn't Prove Its Cruel Border Policy Deters Migration." Just Security. 12 July 2018.

[3]Mehta, Dhrumil. "Separating Families at the Border Is Really Unpopular." FiveThirtyEight. 19 June 2018; Morin, Rebecca. "Poll: 66% of US. Voters Oppose Family Separation." Politico. 18 June 2018; Cordero, Carrie F., Heidi Li Feldman, and Chimène Keitner. "The Law Against Family Separation." *Columbia Human Rights Law Review* 51.2 (2020): 432–508;

Rye, Reilly. "Family Separation Under the Trump Administration: Applying an International Criminal Law Framework." *The Journal of Criminal Law and Criminology* 110, no. 2 (2020): 349–77.

[4]Miller, Devin. "AAP a Leading Voice Against Separating Children, Parents at Border." *AAP News*, American Academy of Pediatricians. 14 June 2018; Linton, Julie M. et al. "Detention of Immigrant Children." *Pediatrics* 139.5 (2017): 1–13. Reaffirmed November 2022.

[5]Habbach, Hajar. "'You Will Never See Your Child Again': The Persistent Psychological Effects of Family Separation." Physicians for Human Rights. February 2020.

[6]Gee, Dylan. "I Study Kids Who Were Separated from Their Parents. The Trauma Could Change Their Brains Forever." Vox. 20 June 2018; "USA: Policy of Separating Children from Parents Is Nothing Short of Torture." Amnesty International. 18 June 2018; Lee, Stephen. "Family Separation as Slow Death." *Columbia Law Review* 119, no. 8 (2019): 2319–84; Satterthwaite, Meg, and Rebecca Riddell. "Arbitrary Detention of Asylum Seekers Perpetuates the Torture of Family Separation." Just Security, Reiss Center on Law and Security, New York University School of Law. 21 June 2019; Brigitte L., Robert Y. Shapiro, and Yaeli Bloch-Elkon. "Donald Trump: Aggressive Rhetoric and Political Violence." *Perspectives on Terrorism* 14, no. 5 (2020): 2–25; Condon, Jenny-Brooke. "When Cruelty Is the Point: Family Separation as Unconstitutional Torture." *Harvard Civil Rights-Civil Liberties Law Review* 56.1 (2021): 37–76; United Nations Standard Minimum Rules for the Treatment of Prisoners ("The Nelson Mandela Rules"). UN General Assembly. Ratified 17 December 2015.

[7]U.S. Congress, House of Representatives, Committee on the Judiciary, "The Trump Administration's Family Separation Policy: Trauma, Destruction, and Chaos," Majority Staff Report, October 2020: 2, 7–10; Sinha, Anita. "An American History of Separating Families." American Constitution Society. 2 November 2020.

[8]U.S. Congress, House of Representatives, Committee on the Judiciary, "The Trump Administration's Family Separation Policy: Trauma, Destruction, and Chaos." Majority Staff Report. October 2020: 4.

[9]U.S. Congress, House of Representatives, Committee on the Judiciary, "The Trump Administration's Family Separation Policy: Trauma, Destruction, and Chaos." Majority Staff Report. October 2020: 4.

[10]"Separated Children Placed in Office of Refugee Resettlement Care." U.S. Department of Health and Human Services, Office of General Inspector. January 2019.

[11]Riordan Seville, Lisa and Hannah Rappleye. "Trump Admin Ran 'Pilot Program' for Separating Migrant Families in 2017." NBC News. 29 June 2018; Soboroff, Jacob and Julia Ainsley. "Trump administration identifies at least 1,700 additional children it may have separated." NBC News. 18 May 2019; U.S. Department of Health & Human Services, Office of Inspector General. "HHS OIG Issue Brief." January 2019.

[12]U.S. Congress, House of Representatives, Committee on Oversight and Reform, "Child Separations by the Trump Administration," Staff Report, July 2019; Sarat, Austin and Dennis Aftergut. "The Trump Officials Who Took Children from Their Parents Should Be Prosecuted." *The Guardian.* 6 September 2022; Dias, Isabela. "The Ongoing Horror of Donald Trump's Family Separation Policy." *Mother Jones.* 18 October 2024.

[13]U.S. House of Representatives, Committee on Oversight and Reform. "Child Separations by the Trump Administration." July 2019.

[14]Harmon, Amy. "Did the Trump Administration Separate Immigrant Children From Parents and Lose Them?" *The New York Times.* 28 May 2018; U.S. Department of Health & Human Services. "Statement of Steven Wagner, Acting Assistant Secretary, Administration for Children and Families, U.S. Department of Health and Human Services." Permanent Subcommittee on Investigations Committee on Homeland Security and Governmental Affairs, United States Senate. 26 April 2018.

[15]Hesson, Ted. "Close to 1,000 Migrant Children Separated by Trump Yet to Be Reunited with Parents." Reuters. 2 February 2023; Bennett, Geoff. "Hundreds of Migrant Children Remain Separated from Families Despite Push to Reunite Them." PBS News. 6 February 2023.

[16]"Family Separation—A Timeline." Southern Poverty Law Center. 23 March 2022.

[17]Carpenter, Zöe. "Democrats Confront the Horror at the Border." *The Nation.* 26 June 2019; Lind, Dara. "The Horrifying Conditions Facing Kids in Border Detention, Explained." Vox. 26 June 2019.

[18]Lind, Dara. "The Horrifying Conditions Facing Kids in Border Detention, Explained." Vox. 26 June 2019.

[19]Haag, Matthew. "Thousands of Immigrant Children Said They Were Sexually Abused in U.S. Detention Centers, Report Says." *The New York Times.* 17 February 2019; Long, Colleen. "At least 4,500 Abuse Complaints at Migrant Children Shelters." AP News. 26 February 2019; Gonzales, Richard. "Sexual Assault of Detained Migrant Children Reported in the Thousands Since 2015." National Public Radio. 26 February 2019; Owens, Caitlin, Stef W. Kight, and Harry Stevens. "Thousands of Migrant Youth Allegedly Suffered Sexual Abuse in U.S. Custody." Axios. 26 February 2019. Also see Endnote 2.

[20]Grabell, Michael and Sanders, Topher. "Immigrant Youth Shelters: 'If You're a Predator, It's a Gold Mine.'" ProPublica. 27 July 2018.

[21]"Room for Hope." International Detention Coalition, 2020; Shepherd, Katie. "Making the Case for Ending Immigration Detention." Immigration Impact 11 November 2020.

[22]Murguia, Sophie. "The Answer to the Family Separation Crisis Is Right There in Front of Us." *Mother Jones.* 29 June 2018; "The Family Case Management Program: Why Case Management Can and Must Be Part of the US Approach to Immigration." Women's Refugee Commission, 2019.

[23]U.S. House of Representatives. Committee on Oversight and Reform and Subcommittee on Civil Rights and Civil Liberties. "The Trump Administration's Mistreatment of Detained Immigrants: Deaths and Deficient Medical Care by For-Profit Detention Contractors." 2020.

[24]Nacos, Brigitte L., Robert Y. Shapiro, and Yaeli Bloch-Elkon. "Donald Trump: Aggressive Rhetoric and Political Violence." *Perspectives on Terrorism* 14, no. 5 (2020): 2–25.

Chapter 11: We the People

[1]"CBP Enforcement Statistics Fiscal Year 2021." U.S. Customs and Border Protection.

[2]Van Fossen, Emily. "MPP Has Created A Refugee Camp in Mexico—Why Aren't We Treating It Like One?" Niskanen Center. 10 February 2019; Mukpo, Ashoka. "Asylum-Seekers Stranded in Mexico Face Homelessness, Kidnapping, and Sexual Violence." American Civil Liberties Union. 18 September 2019; Canetti, Chloe. "Migrant Protection Protocols (MPP)." U.S. Committee for Refugees and Immigrants. October 2021. Rosenberg, Mica. "Border Refugees." Reuters. 23 September 2021; "UNICEF Statement on the Reimplementation of Migrant Protection Protocols, 'Remain in Mexico Policy.'" UNICEF. 9 December 2021.

[3]Burke, Terri. "Chaos and Cruelty for Immigrants Held in Brownsville, Texas." American Civil Liberties Union of Texas. 20 June 2018; Serwer, Adam. "The Cruelty Is the Point." *The Atlantic.* 3 October 2018; *Cashing on Cruelty: Stories of Death, Abuse and Neglect at the GEO Immigration Detention Facility in Aurora.* American Civil Liberties Union of Colorado. 17 September 2019.

[4]Minian, Ana. "1930s: Repatriation of Mexicans." Stanford University, Department of History. 25 June 2020; "Immigration and Relocation in U.S. History." U.S. Library of Congress; Gratton, Brian, and Emily Merchant. "Immigration, Repatriation, and Deportation: The Mexican-Origin Population in the United States, 1920–1950." *The International Migration Review* 47. 4 (2013): 944–75; Balderrama, Francisco E. "The Deportation-Repatriation Campaign Against La Raza." In *In Defense of La Raza: The Los Angeles Mexican Consulate and the Mexican Community, 1929 to 1936,* 15–36. University of Arizona Press, 1982.

[5]Gellman, Irwin F. "The 'St. Louis' Tragedy." *American Jewish Historical Quarterly* 61, no. 2 (1971): 144–56; Konovitch, Barry J. "The Fiftieth Anniversary of the 'St. Louis': What Really Happened." *American Jewish History* 79, no. 2 (1989): 203–9.

[6]"The Federal Reserve's Interactions with Japanese Americans during WWII (1942–1945)." U.S. Federal Reserve. 15 August 2023; "Japanese American Incarceration." The National WWII Museum; Irons, Peter. *Justice at War: The Story of the Japanese-American Internment Cases.* University of California Press, 1993; Hane, Mikiso. "Wartime Internment." *The Journal of American History* 77. 2 (1990): 569–75; Kunioka, Todd T., and Karen M. McCurdy.

"Relocation and Internment: Civil Rights Lessons from World War II." *PS: Political Science and Politics* 39, no. 3 (2006): 503–11.

[7]García, Mario T. "Operation Wetback: The Mass Deportation of Mexican Undocumented Workers in 1954." *The Public Historian* 3, no. 2 (1981): 121–25; Calavita, Kitty. *Inside the State: The Bracero Program, Immigration, and the I.N.S.* Routledge, 1992.

[8]Androff, David K., and Kyoko Y. Tavassoli. "Deaths in the Desert: The Human Rights Crisis on the U.S.-Mexico Border." *Social Work* 57.2 (2012): 165–73; De León, J., Gokee, C., amd Schubert, A. "'By the Time I Get to Arizona': Citizenship, Materiality, and Contested Identities Along the US-Mexico Border." *Anthropological Quarterly* 88.2 (2015), 445–479; Slack, Jeremy, Daniel E. Martínez, Alison Elizabeth Lee, and Scott Whiteford. "The Geography of Border Militarization: Violence, Death and Health in Mexico and the United States." *Journal of Latin American Geography* 15.1 (2016): 7–32; Ewing, Walter A. "'Enemy Territory': Immigration Enforcement in the US-Mexico Borderlands." *Journal on Migration and Human Security* 2.3 (2014): 198–222.

[9]Devereaux, Ryan. "The Border Patrol Calls Itself a Humanitarian Organization. A New Report Says That's a Lie." The Intercept. 3 February 2021; "US: Border Deterrence Leads to Deaths, Disappearances." Human Rights Watch. 26 June 2024.

[10]De León, Jason. *The Land of Open Graves: Living and Dying on the Sonoran Desert Migrant Trail.* Berkeley: University of California Press, 2015.

[11]Warren, Robert, and J.R. Warren. "Unauthorized Immigration to the United States: Annual Estimates and Components of Change, by State, 1990 to 2010." *International Migration Review* 47.2 (2013): 296–329; "Executive Summary, Estimates of the Unauthorized Immigrant Population Residing in the United States: 1990 to 2000." U.S. Immigration and Naturalization Service. January 31, 2003; "Estimates of the Unauthorized Immigrant Population Residing in the United States: 1990 to 2000." U.S. Immigration and Naturalization Service, Office of Policy and Planning; Hoefer, Michael, Nancy Rytina, and Bryan C. Baker. "Estimates of the Unauthorized Immigrant Population Residing in the United States: January 2010." U.S. Department of Homeland Security, Office of Immigration Statistics. February 2011. Baker, Bryan, and Robert Warren. *Estimates of the Unauthorized Immigrant Population Residing in the United States: January 2018–January 2022.* U.S. Department of Homeland Security, Office of Homeland Security Statistics. April 2024.

[12]Camarota, Steven A., and Karen Zeigler. "The Foreign-Born Share and Number at Record Highs in February 2024." Center for Immigration Studies. 28 March 2024; "Mass Deportation: Devastating Costs to America, Its Budget and Economy." American Immigration Council. 24 October 2024.

[13]"The Cost of Immigration Enforcement and Border Security." American Immigration Council. August 2024: 5.

[14]Annual Report: Fiscal Year 2024. U.S. Immigration and Customs Enforcement. 19 December 2024; "Fiscal Year 2024 Bill Summary: Homeland

Security." Homeland Security. House Appropriations Committee Democrats; "Homeland Security, 2024." U.S. Senate Appropriations Committee—Republicans; "The Cost of Immigration Enforcement and Border Security." American Immigration Council. August 2024: 9.

[15]"Rep. Mace Calls for Immediate Fixes: 'Non-Operational Cameras Jeopardize Border Security.'" Office of Congresswoman Nancy Mace. U.S. House of Representatives. 16 October 2024; "The Cost of Immigration Enforcement and Border Security." American Immigration Council. August 2024: 2.

[16]Shane C. Campbell-Staton et al. "Physiological costs of undocumented human migration across the southern United States border." *Science* 374 (2021): 1496–1500. Sigelmann, Laura. "The Hidden Driver: Climate Change and Migration in Central America's Northern Triangle." American Security Project, 2019; Ross, Lindsey R. "Climate Change and Immigration: Warnings for America's Southern Border." American Security Project, 2010; Locke, Justin T. "Climate Change-Induced Migration in the Pacific Region: Sudden Crisis and Long-Term Developments." *The Geographical Journal* 175. 3 (2009): 171–80; Jayawardhan, Shweta. "Vulnerability and Climate Change Induced Human Displacement." *Consilience* 17 (2017): 103–42; Ramos, Erika Pires. "Climate Change, Disasters and Migration: Current Challenges to International Law." *Climate Change: International Law and Global Governance: Volume II: Policy, Diplomacy and Governance in a Changing Environment*, edited by Oliver C. Ruppel, Christian Roschmann, and Katharina Ruppel-Schlichting. Nomos (2013): 739–60; Oberman, Kieran. "Poverty and Immigration Policy." *The American Political Science Review* 109, no. 2 (2015): 239–51; Angelo, Paul J. "Why Central American Migrants Are Arriving at the U.S. Border." Council on Foreign Relations, 2021; Azpuru, Dinorah, and Violeta Hernández. "Migration in Central America: Magnitude, Causes and Proposed Solutions." *Migration and Refugees* (2015): 72–95.

[17]"Communities Affected by Hurricanes Eta and Iota Are Threatened by Food Insecurity, Displacement and the Climate Crisis." International Federation of Red Cross, 11 November 2023; "Central America: 2020 Atlantic Hurricane Season—Situation Report No. 4." United Nations Office for the Coordination of Humanitarian Affairs. 20 November 2020.

[18]"World Bank Annual Report." The World Bank (2024): 50.

[19]"World Migration Report 2024." International Organization for Migration (2024); "International Migration." United Nations, https://www.un.org/en/global-issues/migration.